The Hardworking House

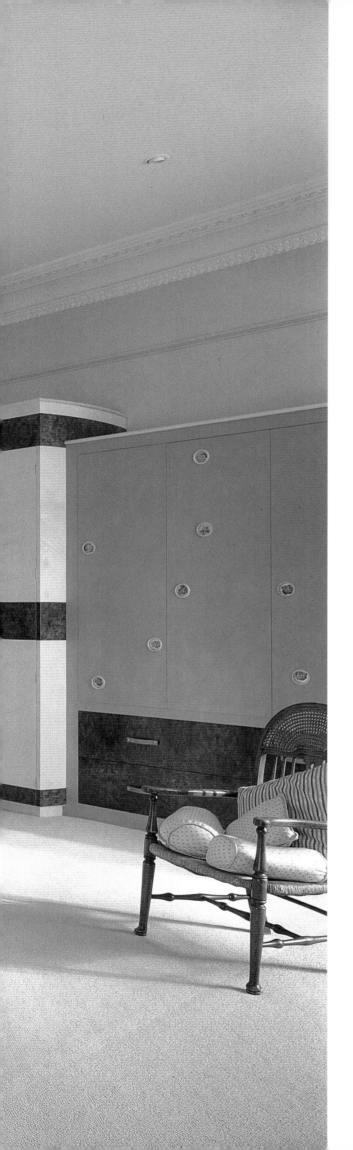

The Hardworking House

THE ART OF LIVING DESIGN

JOHNNY GREY

CASSELL

This edition first published in the UK in 1997 by
Cassell
Wellington House, 125 Strand
London WC2R 0BB

Distributed in the United States
by Sterling Publishing Co., Inc.
387 Park Avenue South,
New York, NY 10016

British Library Cataloguing-in-Publication Data
A catalogue record for this book is available from the British Library

ISBN 0-304-34770-1

Designed by Richard Carr
Edited by Helen Armitage
Picture research by Margaux King and Philippa Lewis
Original colour artwork by Richard Lee
Special photography by James Mortimer and Mark Darley

Printed and bound in Spain

Contents

To Becca, my wife, in the hope that
she will benefit from it

Acknowledgements

I would like to acknowledge the enthusiasm and support of all my clients but, in particular, Tom and Katherine Assheton, Michael and Cathy Levinthal, Hilary and Peter Bazalgette, Sue and Ron Baker, Sir Cameron Mackintosh and Michael Le Poeur Trench, Jim and Lynne Hafner, Howard Winter, David and Alison Streatfeild-James, Felix Dennis, Caroline Jessel, Don and Kirsty Dennes, Nick and Sarah Ross, Carolyn and Nick Balcombe, Johnny and Philippa Paterson, and Howard and Jan Jones, all of whom gave me the opportunity to exercise my skills. I also gratefully acknowledge the hard work of my team: Lynne Fornelies, Richard Lee, David Richards, Mike Rooke and Anna Moore. Special acknowledgements must go as well to the craftspeople who did the work: Jonathan Morriss and his team of supreme furniture-makers including Stephen Cordell, Gordon Hopkins, Jonathan Parlett, Miles Muggleton, Nigel Brown and Patrick Warnes likewise; Paul Jobst for his metal-work; Andrew Parslow for his skills on site; Felix Delmar and Jenny Woods for their painting skills, Paul Saban for his marble and granite work and the many others too numerous to list here. Lastly, but not least, the Australian artist Lucy Turner for her original and highly skilled work on paint and patternwork on so many projects.

Many thanks, too, to the publishing team at Cassell. Chris Fagg for his considerable energy in making the book happen, Rosie Anderson for pulling it together, Helen Armitage for her work on smoothing out my sometimes rather hectic writing, Jane Donovan for helping out and Sarah Chatwin for putting my writing on disk. My thanks, also, to James Mortimer for his superb specialist photography amid sometimes difficult circumstances.

I would also like to acknowledge my good friends in the USA: Kevin Henry for his support and David Peer at European Country Kitchens, Far Hills, New Jersey, now my partner in the United States, who took the plunge to display my work and offer it up to the American public.

INTRODUCTION

THE idea of the hardworking house, a house that is both efficient and enduring, came as an intuitive response to the excesses of the eighties; to the need for a more moral, pragmatic and clear personal environment, free of the stylistic baggage accrued during that decade and closer to our requirements at the end of the twentieth century. The juxtaposition of the two words – hard and work – that separately may have unpleasant connotations might not be considered the best starting-point for the broad coalition of ideas that form the basis of this book. But I use work not just to mean labour but to signify a well-oiled machine as well. As something that implies a satisfying continuity and a sense of order; of life going on with a comforting predictability, confirming that we have some control over our world. This is especially relevant in our own home or private dominion.

The ethos of hard work may be religious in origin – and might have suited the interests of early religious founders – but the reason it remains so strongly embedded in our culture is that it suits our personal and national self-interest. It compounds self-respect and personal prosperity and satisfies the instinct for individual creativity. A key part of this is all the activities that concern nest-building or homemaking. For a man, symbolically, the house is a protective outside shell; for a woman it is a soft and welcoming interior.

The element of self-respect in homemaking is important because it allows room for the notions of economy and self-reliance, enabling us to be independent. This makes us feel efficient and engenders a high sense of self-worth. A well-run household is still a vital part of a successful home life, and a hard-working, well-planned house its natural corollary. It feels good when a household works well, because a sense of order prevails and allows family life to be played out fully. An orderly household provides the vital and solid inner core from which to launch ourselves into the public domain of the outside world.

It is obvious that the house or machine has to work hard, but the way in which we want it to perform for us is something that we can choose ourselves. We are all both householders and potential designers. We not only live in a house or apartment, but we also choose the fabric of the interior and the activities that take place within it. Both its interior and exterior have constantly to perform a wide variety of tasks, on many different levels. The outside must cope with the effects of temperature, water and sound, as well as provide physical security; the inside should give the body support in a wide range of human activity and facilitate nourishment of all kinds. Living in comfort, with a degree of privacy, a strong sense of personal identity, and space for storage, all facilitate the daily tasks of life and provide a backdrop for the theatre of family life.

I often think of each room as a stage for the acting out of a 'play', with characters making their exits and entrances, speaking their parts and moving on. So much happens internally, and the structure of any building must allow for

ABOVE
The effects of age and wear provide a sense of grace and continuity in the choice of materials and their means of execution in this sixteenth-century English house. Good design needs literally to anticipate the coming of age and accept it, as well as, where necessary, the need for maintenance.

OPPOSITE
Palazzo Davanzati (fifteenth-century), Florence. Clean, no-nonsense design in these working parts of the house symbolizes a sense of order and comforting predictability in daily use, as well as confirming its male association with security and protection. They remind me how tough the hardware of a house needs to be to last.

9

this to happen. If this machine for living were anthropomorphized, it would have to become a wise and strong and exceedingly resilient superhuman being. The sheer number of household gods and their domains given by the ancient Greeks and Romans to look after the house bears witness to this. In some ways the house, especially the interior, is an extension of the self, a projection of our thoughts, dreams, actions and personal history, as well as our unconscious absorption of them.

How to make ourselves comfortable at home is one of the major themes of this book. And comfort must include workability – making it easy or enjoyable to carry out the tasks and pleasures of domestic life. In the closed company of a household it is necessary to allow for shared use of space, as well as intimate areas for privacy and quietness. This is where design comes in to form one of the other themes of the book: how to make the interior perform well for us.

It is not so much a new role that we need for the house as a changing awareness of our expectations for our living-quarters. The house as a nest is the fundamental starting-point. It is a basic instinct for people to seek shelter

The room as a stage set is particularly apt for the dining room. This example is a design that I made for a family in north London. The hardworking house doesn't mean a place devoid of comfort – psychological or physical. Quite the reverse. It should suggest the capacity for use.

and to make a structure to provide this. But for most of us in Western society the basic physical elements of shelter are taken for granted with a plentiful supply of housing stock. We have achieved this by now, broadly speaking, for at least a century. What occupies our attention in the twentieth century is comfort psychology, fine tuning for comfort, crudely encompassed by the twin disciplines of technology, on the one hand, and psychology on the other. By this I mean those psychological elements that are present in our physical surroundings and the way in which they speak to us. Why choose one chair, table or lamp over another? We attach personal observations to the real or imagined meaning of furnishings, interior design and architecture. Some people may call this 'style', seen as a whimsical and shallow spur-of-the-moment choice, but there is more depth and richness to our selection of objects, the interior design of our houses and the types of buildings in which we live. They tell a story for us and to us; enable us to create a kind of psychological web that connects us to our house and our self-image. Through this we can explain the full meaning of what really is meant by the word home – something I cover in greater detail in the Hidden House section of chapter 1, 'The Idea of the House'.

There is a need for a down-to-earth examination of all this after the excesses of the eighties and its obsession with style. I am not denigrating the attempt to be stylish; I enjoy those discussions and see a real need for them. I would just caution against style being too high a percentage of the design equation and avoid getting carried too far away from pragmatism, a sense of modesty and what can be executed with vigour and to a high standard. Don't despair if all this sounds too obsessed with the intellectual or the moral, because *The Hardworking House* has a celebratory side too. Human beings have created so many wonderful things, especially for use in everyday domestic life, that it is good to be reminded of them every so often. We can then reappraise them for ourselves and introduce new ways of seeing and understanding the many remarkable objects, interiors and buildings that we have created. So much thought, effort and ingenuity goes into their making that it is worth reappreciating. It is my hope that I can help to do that here.

Although *The Hardworking House* concentrates more on abstract ideas and concepts rather than a specific shopping list of style solutions, I have tried to balance the inspirational with the practical, the spiritual with the intellectual, the historical with the contemporary, the traditional with the modern, the grand ideas with the detail and the imaginary with the useful. Whole books have been written on design philosophy by innumerable architects and designers, often with rather over-inflated and high-flown ideas. My offering aims to be more accessible, with an attempt to justify and explain the use of designers in the home. There has been a popular reaction against them for some years, often because they tend to take over what are essentially our homes, turning them into showpieces as opposed to places in which to live. Good designers are mindful of going too far, but the temptation is always there, and it a difficult balancing act to get right. So, why employ one?

Palazzo Davanzati, Florence. There is a need for a softer, feminine quality to offset the male dominance inherent in the earlier history of the home as a 'castle'. Beauty has a part in our idea of home, softening its hard surfaces and 'male' environment and plays a role in providing a sense of grace and comfort, as demonstrated in the hand-painted walls of this fifteenth-century palazzo bathroom.

The kitchen is the room where most design assistance is necessary. In the room-by-room section, a short review of its sociable history is included, together with ways of seeing kitchens in a new light. Five examples are shown, including the one illustrated here, designed at the cutting edge of technological innovation for a house in Palo Alto, California.

Designers are most useful in all the rooms where we need technical assistance. Also planning space, often to very precise requirements, and trying to derive maximum use from it can only be obtained with the help of someone who has developed the necessary skills. I believe the kitchen to be the room where design assistance is the most necessary, so I've dealt with that in some detail. The bathroom, too, is a demanding space with its capacity for deterioration through the effects of water. Until recently it was neither appreciated as a room with much potential for leisure and enjoyment, nor deemed worthy of any design input. Public areas, such as corridors, staircases, hallways, laundry/utility rooms and now the newly emerging need for a media or soundproof room, often benefit from the skills of a designer to make them work properly.

There are problems finding designers with bona-fide skills in domestic design. In many respects, a new profession of home designers needs to evolve. Architects have an excellent training that is perhaps the most suitable, but their scale tends to be larger than is appropriate for the minutiae of domestic interior design. It is concerned more with the outside, and overall space and structure. Architects can be retrained to enjoy this smaller, more concentrated scale of domestic work. I put myself through this, having trained originally as an architect. But I had a predisposition towards the small scale, particularly an attachment to furniture, and the process of making things, which made it easy for me. An interest in ergonomics, craftsmanship and materials, and how people use their interiors and fittings is another key requisite for interior design.

Among the illustrations in the book there are many examples of projects I have attempted to realize or had built, and the captions help to explain their basic idea and purpose. But there is also an entire chapter – 'Five Contemporary Designers' Solutions' – devoted to the work of some of the world's most thoughtful and inventive designers and architects, who are influencing the future through their new approaches. They each have highly individual ways of working an extraordinary variety in their palette of materials with their own thoroughly unique and coherent design philosophies. I have tried to summarize some of their key ideas.

In the history of the hardworking house I have selected a few specific historical antecedents that underpin the concept. There are many more, especially if the study is widened beyond Western culture. This is not my intention here, but that doesn't mean they don't have equal validity or interest.

The short section on missing rooms is an attempt to remind us that new ideas for rooms are a welcome response to the changing way we live. In most houses rooms undergo a change of use frequently, and in minor ways they alter as the people in them vary their activity, even on a daily or hourly basis. My original family home on the Sussex Downs was a smallholding with a two-bedroom cottage and two barns. We rebuilt one of the barns and called it the New Barn. Its pattern of use was the story of our family's progress. At first it was an outdoor bedroom, then a music room that alternated as a dining room and teenage party space. When my eldest brother, Rupert, and I set up

an antiques business to help pay for our university expenses, it became a showroom. On cold days it doubled as an indoor workshop. As it had a loft, this still continued in use as a sleeping place.

When I established my first furniture-making business, Sussex Woodwork, the New Barn became an office. A few years later after the company had moved out, my youngest brother, Christopher, housed his furniture there and used it as his English base while he was studying in Provence. Shortly afterwards Rupert took over the whole property, and it became a dark room for his photographic pursuits as well as a study, the loft being used to store his photographic records and other valuable junk that he could not quite give to Oxfam. And this list doesn't include the few years I used it as a design studio, or as a dining-room for special occasions.

This is the story of a hardworking room over a 15-year timescale. I suspect there are many others like it; in fact every house needs at least one or two such spaces. We called it New Barn because when we arrived at the property it had collapsed, and so we rebuilt it. But I often wondered if we could have found a more accurate name for it, based on a description of its function – the back-up room, the flexible room, or the work room? Perhaps it should have been the room with no name, in which any activity was permitted. I think now, though, that a fair description would be the hardworking room.

Johnny Grey
Rogate, Petersfield, Hampshire, UK/Far Hills, New Jersey, USA

A view of my brother Rupert's Library Barn known as 'The New Barn' had several uses, which changed regularly, thus a non-specific name was appropriate.

1

THE

IDEA

OF THE

HOUSE

A kitchen installed in Kensington, London, using Soft Geometry, where the circular island drum for food preparation acts as a fulcrum around which the rest of the furniture, including the circular sink cabinet, is planned.

The Hardworking House

BELOW
Making the entrance area work involves a combination of technical skills: mastering pedestrian traffic flow, taking account of personal idiosyncrasies and conveying the right kind of messages, both subliminal and real, to incoming visitors. In this London flat the architect Jeremy Cockayne manipulates the space ingeniously, with the skill of a feng shui expert.

OPPOSITE
With the wider range of materials now available and our greater exposure to the skills of craftspeople one realizes how much opportunity there is for creativity. Here an innovatory technique with concrete by Buddy Rhodes allows its use in countertops and floors.

I have worked as a designer on houses for nearly 20 years on over 200 projects. Having completed *The Art of Kitchen Design* (1994), I wanted to write a similar book for the whole house. I have come to realize that there is much more to the design of a house interior than just to follow the architect's plans, make furniture, decide on colour schemes and all the related minutiae that need to be worked out. One requires input from a wide variety of sources – from clients, the immediate environment and the cultural and historical climate, as well as the world of the imagination. But I have also discovered that the accumulation of knowledge and technique is tremendously important – from craft techniques, through understanding the technical maze of building, to the ways in which we move around and use space.

When I visit a client for the first time I am regularly surprised by the poor use they often make of their space; how it could be organized so much more efficiently and enjoyably. Doors in the wrong place, a lack of natural light or access to the garden, unsatisfactory lighting, ill-conceived bathrooms or kitchens unergonomically designed are all frequent design flaws. The build-up of years of experience in solving practical problems, based on understanding construction techniques, materials and a study of home ergonomics is vital, but so is developing an awareness of the hidden or psychological elements necessary to make houses comfortable. These are two key themes running through this book. The third side of the design triangle is the imagination that acts equally as a kind of glue, communication device and homing instinct that leads us unerringly to the right place. By practising along these lines as a designer, I have developed tremendous affection for the whole design process.

When you visit old houses, where the effects of age are visible in their fabric, there is a wonderful sense of peace and reassurance. The effects of both time and evident use produce a unique reverence, like the worn down threshold at the door of an old church. This is what I aspire to in my work, and I suspect it is something for which other designers and architects also aim. To produce work of value that will endure, hence the hardworking house – a home that is durable and works well.

However, there are other purposes implied in the use of the book's title. I want also to show appreciation for the idea of the house, both in our minds and in reality. A variety of designs as great in number and as individual as the people who live in them stand as a testimony to the creative genius of mankind and a celebration of an inner spirit. All those wonderful materials that have been provided for us to use – wood, stone, clay, glass, metal, silk, wool, paint to name but some – add up to an extraordinary palette. In my more spiritual moments I think it an awesome responsibility to make sure these materials are used with care and respect, not only not to waste them but also to celebrate them with fine craftsmanship and good design. These are activities on which I

particularly concentrate in my work. I practise as designer rather than a decorator or architect. I focus on what I have termed the hardworking rooms of the house, which is where most people need design assistance.

Every house is different. Old houses, in particular, which were not planned tightly or have been subsequently extended, often have unexpected or eccentric parts with surplus space that encourage incidental or unexpected use. These unplanned spaces often attract people to a house. As irrational elements these features are unlikely to be designed into new housing, which, for this reason, is often considered to lack character.

American architect and writer Christopher Alexander is one practitioner who has made allowances for the quirks. Luckily for us he has written the classic architecture and planning textbook, *A Pattern Language*, first published in 1977. It is a remarkable treatise and an invaluable manual for those of us who wish to design or adapt our own houses. Alexander offers a cornucopia of practical ideas that can make a house not only function well on an everyday basis but respond to the human spirit too. It is not obscure, and the humility of tone adopted, often low key and in plain English, means that it can be used by everyone.

From Alexander we can begin to build up a picture of a comfortable yet practical, busy but welcoming house, where the design aids activity and enhances the sociability of those who live in it, while preserving privacy, encouraging creativity and providing the building with character and atmosphere.

An example of Christopher Alexander's first project, completed at West Dean College in Sussex. He employs indigenous materials – here the use of cut flints, found in local chalk deposits, continues a local tradition – and traditional techniques, as did the Arts and Crafts movement. Both advocate buildings that belong. The same applies with interiors, which should be private yet sociable, practical yet soulful, allowing yet containing the character of the house and those who live there.

This is, in my opinion, a way of describing a hardworking house. It may sound a bit like a description of a Mediterranean or Greek island village house, but Christopher Alexander and his team were based in Berkeley, California, and his ideas were aimed at redressing the lack of soul and practicality in Western house building and urban planning in the mid-to-late twentieth century. It is not architects or designers who are totally at fault here, although they must share the blame. It is more that our vision as a society – our ideas of what we need, what our priorities are, what makes us feel comfortable – needs to mature.

It is no accident that many of the houses we admire, especially in Europe, are old. They were assembled carefully by local craftsmen to an individual's specific requirements – often over a long period during which definite building patterns were established. The person who commissioned the house would live in it. The communication process was clear and short. In the twentieth century few of us build or commission our own houses. Developers act as second-hand long-distance clients, and builders are seldom local or committed in any emotional way to the end result. The role of design is minimal. There is no guardian for enforcing high standards, and scant acknowledgement of the subtle or hard-won knowledge or 'humane' input that a designer can provide.

The only way most of us can connect fully with our house is to refurbish, adapt and maintain its interior and its garden. This is why I have decided to concentrate so much on the interior for this book. But this need not be seen only as a second-best option either. There is something deeply satisfactory and enjoyable about restoring a house or giving it a new lease of life, about bringing in fresh ideas and improvements that can be tangibly measured.

There is something deeply satisfying and enjoyable about restoring an old house and giving it a new lease of life; about bringing in fresh ideas and improvements that can be measured tangibly. Here an opening has been created between two rooms, facilitating movement and communication and increasing light levels; the curved cupboard, accessed from both spaces, now links the room together.

19

Constant Change:
Fashion, Style and Sociology

ABOVE
Fashion is necessary, as it stimulates change, not only as a way of climbing out of some terrible periods of design (it took us into them too) but also as expression for successive generations. We can now look at a sixties' interior as history and enjoy it for its sense of newness.

OPPOSITE
Eric Owen Moss's Lawson–Westen house, completed in 1993, in California. As radical as the sixties' interior of its time and still concerned with modernity, it is more accomplished in its materials, shapes and architectural skills.

I F we now lived inside the house of the future as projected by the prevailing intellectual ideas in the 1950s, 1960s and even the 1970s, I suspect we would all be feeling rather uncomfortable, stripped of cultural clutter, our houses based on serving only our functional needs. In an exhibition entitled *Italy: The New Domestic Landscape* at the Museum of Modern Art, New York, in 1972, designers were asked to create rooms of the future. An unstated axiom of their schemes was that we do not need any emotional connection to our house, furniture, or everyday objects. These are merely consumables, disposable and easily replaced by a new or better model. On a more pragmatic note there was the fully fitted, multi-purpose space, where the wall-to-wall furniture – 'modular and fully flexible' – was made from plastic resin and could presumably be delivered complete anywhere in the world from a mail-order catalogue. Rational and flexible – but only to manufacture, not once installed! What followed in reality wasn't any better. The fitted kitchens made of laminate plastic were rigid, geometric and soul-less places and indicate what the market place had to offer.

Thank goodness the future has turned out differently! Admittedly we have had to live through Post-Modernism with its clapped-on styling, but it has taken us along the right road, even if perhaps recently we have taken a wrong turning. At the end of the decade, in 1979, I wrote a design manifesto, of which a condensed version was published as 'In Place of Modernism' in *Design Magazine* (1981). It was a modest attempt to work out my own alternative philosophy to the poverty of the Modern Movement, which dominated the architectural scene during that decade. The manifesto was a plea to understand the non-material elements in design. It incorporated the influence of new academic disciplines such as the study of semiotics, the idea that all man-made objects are signs or symbols and bear a wider meaning than just their material content.

I felt comfortable with this. I argued strongly that it should form the basis of a new vocabulary or form, of a language of ornament that could allow the participation of artists and crafts people, of history and local cultural tradition in the design and manufacture of objects for everyday life. These ideas are now old hat. Anti-Modernist deviations such as period features, ethnic styles, individualism and retro-styling are all commonplace and raise little controversy. Now there is a prevailing tolerance, a plethora of design influences running through popular taste even among the more highbrow design élite. I find the late twentieth century a healthier period in which to design, for there is more freedom to be creative, more enjoyment of individual elements such as furniture and the paraphernalia of history and everyday life.

OPPOSITE
In my own kitchen, converted from a garage, the preparation area occupies only 40 per cent of the floor space. The remainder of the room is devoted to a comfortable and sociable lounging area, provided by the sofa, an integrated dining area, and a play space for our four children. This is typical of recent kitchen divisions of space.

BELOW
Generous kitchen space in Eric Owen Moss's Lawson–Westen House (1993). The focus is the central island, inherently sociable as activity is brought into the centre of the room, not facing the wall.

Fashion continues to play its part; in many ways a healthy one. But in interior design and furnishing, caution and tradition still enjoy a major role in the decoration of the house. Furniture has a long lifespan and is more expensive than ephemeral articles, such as clothes; equally, built-in architectural fittings, for kitchens and bathrooms, for example, are not cheap and disposable items. Fabrics, however, are changed more easily and readily, and so are more subject to fashion trends. But what of the general planning and the overall design of the house interior?

The principal change is seen in the kitchen, a room currently on the ascendant. It has become the king of the house; it is a communal and multi-purpose space that is, ultimately, for many its main sociable room. The major new arrival is, or will be, the media room. With 'home theatres', surround-sound systems and the enduring popularity of contemporary rock/pop music, there is a real need for soundproof rooms. In northern climates the advantages of a conservatory, or sun room, are now recognized. Autumn and spring sun, as well as heat gain, make the conservatory a viable and economical way of extending the ground-floor area.

One of the least-understood demands upon a house – and perhaps the hardest of which to adapt because of the permanent nature of bricks and mortar – is the effects of the pace at which family circumstances change. 'The Seven Ages of Man', Shakespeare's adage, has stood the test of time. Well enough to be of

some use to us when analysing how to design our house. Almost every act of behaviour can be shown to relate to chronological age, concurs David Carter, author of *Psychology for Architects* (1974). Homes evolve as life does. Joan Kron in her excellent book *Home Psyche* (1985), the social psychology of home decoration, considers age a key issue in determining what support and comfort we need from our environment. Houses, or at least the uses to which they are put, never stand still.

But what of the general thrust; of future trends? Writing this book in 1997, it seems impossible that changes won't come with the massive upheavals caused by the arrival of the information age. Wider dissemination of knowledge must cause the breakdown of cultural barriers and a move towards the notion of 'one world', a concept now acknowledged in the contemporary music scene. World music, so why not world design? Probably we'll hang on to many of our more long-standing cultural habits. But ethnic design, as documented by Dinah Hall (1993) in her best-selling book of that title, provides a rich resource for simple and unspoilt ideas, inspired by local traditions and in response to specific functional needs, such as, for example, the variation of woodworkers' hand tools. It needn't be ethnic either. Hi-tech has crossed all cultural borders. Beneath its sillier manifestation as a fashion-style lies an appealing attempt at honesty to material and sheer enjoyment of process. Fine engineering, the expressed perfection of each component, provides visible elegance of construction and economy of material and takes sensible advantage of mass production.

The greatest shift is in the world of work. As Charles Handy outlines in his book, *The Empty Raincoat* (1994), there is change in where, how, and what to do. Working at home will surely affect a major proportion of the population. Downsizing by the big multi-nationals into smaller units and using self-employed consultants, assembled for specific projects, is already happening. It may turn out to be a thoroughly civilizing development, adding quality to marital and family relationships, reducing the wastage of travel time and making for a more independent existence. The job for life at the office or factory is almost over. Ever more home-organized work will be feasible by the time great swathes of cable have been laid, not to mention the use of satellite and video phones, the Internet and computerized education services.

In *Out of Control: The New Biology of Machines* (1994) Kevin Kelly predicts that future technological devices and infrastructure will reach the complexity of biological systems. He suggests that a fridge in the year 2045 would dwell in an ecology of other machines – watching the clock, ordering milk before the carton is empty, notifying the local store by phone. Microchips will be embedded in lamps to reflect light needs at any time of the day or night. Already, programmed lighting scenes, or house routes, are being installed in up-market houses in the United States. Choices are on offer, depending on our destination or mood. These developments may not be entirely wholesome or genuinely improve our quality of life, but they do present the opportunity for increasingly sophisticated support from technology. The world outside our home clearly so much affects the inside.

BELOW

In this kitchen I have tried to avoid any obvious cultural references, making the room more a celebration of the very best of craftsmanship and materials. High craft, rather than hi-tech, nevertheless it shares some of the same roots, such as pleasure in fine engineering, bold design and use of material.

OPPOSITE

Philippe Starck blurs the boundaries between good taste and Kitsch, domestic and commercial interiors, fashion and furniture, and between the disciplines of design. The sheer strength and determination of his vision ensures that his work will play an important role in contemporary design, long after any concerns as to whether his ideas may date have been raised.

The Hidden House: *Psychology of the House*

For a house to become a home it needs to provide not just physical comfort but also psychological well-being, although to some extent these are inseparable. We need protection from the elements and from the myriad of unknown people lurking in our shadows, both real and imaginary, the hidden inheritance of our days as prehistoric, marauding tribes.

A HOME FOR THE PSYCHE

Keeping at bay the outside world forms part of a defence mechanism necessary for our survival. We need the opportunity to nurture our inner world for both physiological and psychological reasons. I believe the role of home as a spiritual, emotional and psychological resting-place is of equal importance to its physical part in providing protection from the elements. Our home can be a house standing on the edge of a cliff, but it can still make us feel safe or at ease. The home is like a shell in which we can hide or withdraw from the outside world for safety and self-renewal.

In other words our home is intimately connected to our psyche. Perhaps a house is not a home until the soul is connected to it. Home is where the psyche feels it ultimately belongs. It may not be just a building but a particular landscape, a city, a town or a village or simply a special place. Other elements come in too: friends and family, climate and nationality, customs and language. Over time this psychic comfort zone can change, as people who cross cultural borders know well. Feelings of disturbance and a sense of loss can only be made good by creating new roots and connections. Eventually the passage of time will enable a new psychic field or comfort zone to form.

I don't think we can consciously achieve a home for the psyche. It is only possible to provide the right circumstances, and early on in life this is done for us by our parents. We don't choose our childhood environment. We collect experience of a place whether we like it or not – there isn't much choice over many aspects of our lives. Our psychic intelligence is collected randomly over time, so this comfort zone is curiously resistant to direct influence. In the terms of reference of this book, developing the house into a hardworking, comfortable place must help to keep us healthily connected to our psyche.

Ultimately, the issue of whether or not we feel comfortable within ourselves is one that no amount of good house designing can resolve. But a real home can mitigate or, at least, supply a breathing space to recoup, a chance to refuel and ultimately go forward. All this is done within our mental landscape rather than the material one, and it is the response that we make to a place or building that matters. What previous memories or thought patterns does it trigger? How is our imagination affected?

BELOW
One way of making ourselves feel at home is through the creation of an original design feature. This quirky yet utilitarian staircase, with its hint of enmeshing and integrating spiders' webs, personalizes this room, reminding its occupant that there is nowhere else like it.

OPPOSITE
At Beckley Park, a sixteenth-century Tudor moated manor house near Oxford, the sense of order provided by the view of the topiary highlights the role of the garden as the transition zone, that is nature controlled. The thick stone walls and the small window create a feeling of security. These physical qualities impact on our psychological well-being – factors that are often forgotten about in contemporary houses.

Secrecy plays a role in comfort, as shown in this house (1986–7), Brighton, Sussex, made of chicken wire and cement by architect David Mayhew. In a secret place one can be oneself without interference. An opportunity for privacy defends the source of the well-springs of our personality. Children have easy access through their capacity to daydream. Antonio Gaudí's Casa Battló (1904–17), Barcelona, is a comparable testament to this.

In his renowned, if sometimes obscure, book *The Poetics of Space* (1994) Gaston Bachelard traces the significance of the house in our imagination, reminding us how our thoughts, memories and dreams shape our perception of the house. He claims that the chief benefit of a house is to provide shelter for day-dreaming: 'It allows one to dream in peace.... The house is one of the greatest powers of integration for the thoughts, memories and dreams of mankind.' His point about day-dreaming is interesting because it is different from dreaming, for we guide and influence the process to some extent. It is a part-conscious, part-unconscious expression. The conscious mind, at its most relaxed state, produces alpha rhythms that mix with the deeper states of the unconscious mind and floats between the two. Such a state is both comfortable and potentially useful as the imagination can be partially directed. 'Day-dream values', Bachelard concludes, 'communicate poetically from soul to soul. To read poetry is essentially to day-dream.' Furthermore he says, 'The house, the bedroom, the garret [together] furnished the framework of an intermediate dream, one that poetry alone through the creation of a poetic work could succeed in achieving completely.'

Poetry for Bachelard is presumably the capacity to use words in a way that causes a heightened sense of reality, which set off unanticipated connections. For children, day-dreams occupy a large proportion of their play time. As adults, it is in the day-dream more than recorded memory that childhood remains alive, and the house of our childhood can be recalled. Our first 'house' is, as Bachelard says, our first universe and colours our experience and images of what constitutes familiarity, comfort and our expressions of belonging that stay with us thereafter.

Understanding the psychological significance of the house has been helpfully illuminated by psychoanalysis, especially through dream interpretation. In Artemidorous Daldianus's book *Interpretation of Dreams* (1963), he explains how, in dreams, the house acts as an image of ourselves. The roof may represent the spiritual search for completion; as in real life when the roof is added, the house is finished. The basement represents our primordial or native instincts.

The kitchen, according to Oliver Marc in his fascinating book, *The Psychology of the House* (1977), may be the place where psychic change occurs. The dreamer's movement and the discoveries made there are symbols of ourselves revealed by the unconscious. The outside, or façade, may correspond to the face or appearance of the dreamer. Marc goes on, 'The house is the fullest and oldest manifestation of the psyche. Like dance, like song, it represents a necessity of expression... it provides the necessary base from which consciousness is formed, consolidated and expanded, and the self defined.' The house is the hearth, the common ground of the psyche's growth and transformation. He then talks about the problem of mass standardization of house design and, based on the assumption of the need for individual development of each person's psyche, of how it causes great discomfort. The individuality of the interior of the house seems to be an increasingly necessary antidote to

the outward uniformity of new housing schemes and developments. Individualizing our interior space provides a chance for our inner life to flourish. This gives new purpose and significance to the value of interior design.

As we start to appreciate the significance of the house in dreams, the connection to history and the collective unconscious, we can begin to see its structure, its interior and its exterior, in a new and deeper way. We can become more appreciative of this wonderful shelter, of its purpose and of what it can be when fully realized. We can understand better why we are so attached to our houses. And, conversely, how our houses can be inexpressive, uncomfortable and meaningless places for us where there is little connection to them beyond their offer of transient relief as temporary shelter.

The hidden-house fantasy. Houses need to provide us with an opportunity to hide from the complexities and problems of the outside world and find relief there so that we can refuel and go forth refreshed. The interior design plays its part in this too.

29

The Cultural Umbrella

THE search for individuality in the design and decoration of our homes is the undercurrent running through the previous sections. We can't and don't want to operate in a totally private world, a kind of self-generated vacuum. We are social beings and need to be part of a greater entity. Our psychic connection to this is through the collective unconscious, which, as revealed by Jung, suggests an ancient and deep-rooted connection among all human beings, past and present. Jung discovered common art forms and symbols that separate cultures had developed individually without being aware of the existence of others. The collective unconscious forms a hidden link for us as individuals, providing us with a sense of belonging that underwrites the unspoken meaning and value of cultural activities; it gives us a commonality and, as such, acts like a cultural glue.

The collective unconscious is what makes us feel part of society – in my case the English or European nation and Anglo-Saxon culture – with whatever ethnic, historical group or subculture we identify. It is made real in the world of culture, art and history, and manifests itself individually not only through general self-expression but also in the particular design of our interiors and houses. This is what we are concerned with here, and we draw upon our hidden or submerged interior worlds when we express ourselves through our taste. The collective unconscious provides the hidden thread, most readily accessible through material objects and the history, language, art, architecture, which are all, literally, signs of life. If this seems overcomplicated, it is only because hidden meanings are by definition difficult to reveal. And, although we don't need to analyse everything we do all the time, just occasionally it is useful to do so.

In the early eighties, with the development of the new science of social anthropology, valuable work was done to understand the purpose and motive of social consumption; of why people buy specific goods or identify with certain types of lifestyles and objects. In *World of Goods: Towards an Anthropology of Consumption* (1978), Mary Douglas and Baron Isherwood reveal the secrets of why we relate to certain objects and rely on them as a part of our identity.

I have termed our collective cultural resources the Cultural Umbrella. It provides us with a context from which we can draw to make ourselves connect up with the world outside us. The discovery of our own taste – which can take some while to find – and our capacity to express it comes from

My brother Rupert and I for a few years ran a most enjoyable antique furniture business, discovering much about the history of design, furniture etc first hand. Here in this library-barn are some of the items he kept. Collecting objects from the past links us with it and with our wider cultural heritage, reinforcing our connection with history and making for a sense of comfort and belonging.

continually learning, using and contributing to it. Grounding ourselves within the world of culture, art and history and finding our own taste and the confidence to express it are among the needs of a maturing personality. Once we, as individuals, have achieved a roof over our heads, sufficient food to eat and a stable emotional life, then this is the sphere that gives us sustenance. The American psychologist Abraham Maslow in his seminal *Motivation and Personality* (1954) talks of the self-actualized man, someone who has achieved base physiological satisfaction and is ready for fulfilment through higher or non-physical needs. Whether we are self actualized or happy is measured by ability to enjoy regular peak experiences, which Maslow describes as some event or thought that provides us with a flash of insight or momentary high, with feelings of intense pleasure or happiness. Something that engenders in us a sense of completeness.

The cultural umbrella is also a record of man's achievements, of what we have left behind and what continues. It fills our existence with purpose, meaning and continuity and provides the opportunity for communication and creativity. But how does this relate to the home?

Household objects, furniture, books, gifts, china and general effects are invested with meaning, the making of which is part of our cultural activity. They evoke memories, family connections and a myriad of possible psychological responses. They are a tactile connection to memory. We invest a bit of ourselves in them, constantly retelling our story not only to ourselves but also to others: to our friends, families and visitors. These objects become part of us in a minor way, expressed not only in an entire room or complete interior but also within the whole of the house itself. Through no conscious effect, just the passage of time, our house or apartment will become a home.

The word home is derived from the Old Norse *heimr* and combines a description of place with psychological attributes, such as well-being, contentment and a sense of belonging, regarding the family as individuals and the home as a place of refuge. It is interesting that so much of its meaning rests in the psyche with a fascinating duality in its connection to physical objects. Rather like Proust's madeleine dipped in tea reminding him of things past, so this personal estate of mobile objects that we move around from house to house creates an aura of belonging and familiarity, wherever we are.

I can recall moving into our first house with only a bed, tablelamp and a few saucepans. In the otherwise empty house for the first night, it still felt like home. Minimalists have a point! Dogs have to mark their territory with scent. Maybe we have inherited the behaviour by needing to decorate our interiors with favoured objects. Whatever way we view our personal 'estate', it is an extension of us; equally it is an expression of our own preferences, with a wider cultural significance. The umbrella stretches over us all, connecting us and reinforcing our commonality.

Collecting objects is pleasurable not only because of the sheer enjoyment of accumulation, the pleasure of comparison but also due to the comfort of plenty, which imbues us with a solid sense of security. A house becomes a home when it is full of familiar ornaments and objets that we have put together in our own unique combination.

Popular Ideas

KITSCH: LIBERATION AND RENEWAL

OPPOSITE

With Gaudí's Casa Batlló (1904–17), Barcelona, we can breathe a sigh of relief at his sense of freedom, which shows a truly creative spirit at work. As he stepped outside tradition by dispensing with conventional taste, many contemporaries dismissed his work as vulgar and without merit. Today no visit to Barcelona is complete without at least taking in the extravagant and ornate Church of the Sagrada Familia, started in 1888 and still being worked on.

BELOW

Clever manipulation of ideas of popular low-class objects and ersatz material provide fodder for the new in this startling and original furniture by Charles Rutherfoord.

Kitsch is a German term for 'vulgar trash', a taste that became fashionable in the early twentieth century. Its style – overdecoration, childish colours, whimsical abandonment, lack of intellectual judgement – is often viewed as the mass culture of the ignorant, the sentimental and the lower orders. Upgrading ourselves to a position above those who indulge in such sins is a common response to it. The cultured classes might stand aloof and pronounce themselves pure. In the West, during the sixties, attitudes altered. Popular culture – through the Beatles in music, Andy Warhol in art, the general elevation of working-class culture in literature and film – revealed its underlying strength, originality and talent. True, degradation still takes place by abridging Shakespeare, Disney-style, by sentimentalizing Bavarian castles and by the prevalence of clip-on Louis XVI style gold-plastic handles, but that is a cheap and unsatisfactory way of looking at Kitsch.

The infusion of popular culture into mainstream design accelerated in the late sixties with beneficial effect. Modernism, the twentieth-century art and design movement, was rapidly becoming a high church, to which only the pure and clean were admitted. Allowing no room for ornament or the clutter of human existence, the machine aesthetic denied much of the evidence of real life.

Tradition, order, the role of predominant aesthetic styles, while admirable and much needed architectural disciplines – many inherited from Georgian Anglo-Saxonism – can become a tyranny, creating a design impasse or cultural strait-jacket. In a sense, popular 'values' rescued us. The Beatles helped us unwind on many levels, certainly more than in just musical terms. They became an image for the time because we were due some cultural freedom and liberation from restrictive Victorian rules of behaviour. The levelling effect of the wide appeal of the Beatles' music (anybody who liked a good rhythm), and the implication that anyone could enjoy it – it doesn't have to be highbrow or complex to be good – are ideas that percolated through into the design world.

While popular culture and Kitsch are not one and the same thing, they have strong connections. Kitsch is an unfettered, unselfconscious attempt to deliver simple pleasures in an accessible way, albeit often with sentimentality. There are no taste restrictions, and there is no need to link up with informed 'cultural' opinion to enjoy it. This means that Kitsch is capable of throwing up new icons, in terms of people, phenomena or

When is decoration and ornament acceptable? Here the playful use · of wirework is designed to give sensual pleasure. Its claim to function is limited but so is the role of a picture hanging on a wall. Charles Rutherfoord designed this thoroughly enjoyable flower holder. The home needs objects that provide comfort or sensuality without needing any further explanation.

objects, relatively easily. And because it is unselfconscious – without the sense of veto that is implied in the world of good taste – so it results in a sense of freedom. For many of us the lack of censorship employed by the educated is off-putting, likewise its sentimentality, but this is favourably balanced by other inputs, such as innovation, easy-access 'comfort' values and the sparkle of fashion. I think Kitsch can have a role of renewal by feeding new images into popular culture, which otherwise can be too easily manipulated by interested parties, such as mass-market manufacturers and media multinationals.

In the design world, highbrow design invents new images, which, in similar ways, become sanitized. For example, contemporary French designer Philippe Starck – whose style is an audacious mix of flamboyant forms and visual puns – designs extraordinary curved chairs, which are beautiful and uncompromising, if a little uncomfortable. In a few years a version of his chairs will appear in a department store, somewhat softened and made acceptable to a wider public. This seems acceptable to me, almost the natural order of things.

Historically, there is no monopoly on Kitsch, but the first development of mass culture certainly belongs to the United States, where comfort and convenience have long played more important roles than tradition and respectability. The point at which Kitsch becomes valuable is when it enters backwards into 'high taste' culture, acting as a source of renewal. An example of this is mid-century American architect Bruce Goff. He has combined an extraordinary imagination with an intense interest in using new materials in unconventional ways to make for surprise and impact, excitement and connection with nature. His work is a borderline scenario. Is it serious architecture or is it Kitsch? I have always been fascinated with what he does and find his output daring, inventive and challenging; whether or not I'd like to live in one of his houses, I'm not so sure. But, as with many objects or places with a strong character, I think I might well learn to love it. Apparently many of his clients – as with those of American architect Frank Lloyd Wright – will testify they eventually became attached to their homes, or overcontrolled architect-designed environments, after an ambivalent beginning.

Along the same lines, but now universally adored, is Spanish architect Antonio Gaudí. Ignored for many generations (he worked mostly in the early 1900s), he is no longer, I suspect, considered Kitsch. Gaudí shows the extent to which architectural design relies on crafts people and their skills, their work with their hands and their minds involving a medieval way of building. His approach also stresses the so-called imaginative elements of architecture, such as its sculptural aspects. These help so much to infuse buildings with the abstract qualities of delight, surprise and fantasy that people can relate to easily, ranking them in terms of importance above the more high-faluting qualities of order, classical discipline and such all-round values of apparent good taste.

Gaudí, so James Sweeney and Josep Luis Sert say in their book, *Antonio Gaudí* (1960), dispensed with the concept of taste to avoid being tied to any

one style or 'revival'. One can breathe a sigh of relief at the sense of freedom he must have encountered. It shows a true creative spirit at work. We need no academic qualification to enjoy his work. In some ways his is truly democratic design, because it engenders an emotional response rather than an intellectual one, which is one of the fundamental elements of Kitsch. Gaudí's work finally became properly recognized in the 1970s – a recognition that reminds us how important it is for the public to enjoy and empathize with their built environment.

Two contemporary American designers, Neil Korpinen and Erik Erickson, have flirted with Kitsch in an unusual way – by sitting on an imaginary fence. They have used Kitsch design styles, colours and objects from the forties and fifties in their house in Los Angeles. Full of ambiguity and with an unusual mix of colour, surface and shape, their approach to design is sensuous, evoking feelings of the half-familiar, with overtures to lushness, pattern and homeliness. Their work raises doubts about condemning Kitsch out of hand and challenges popular conceptions about what it is, as well as about what is good taste, comfortable and homely. Loosely described as popular retro, I think Korpinen and Erickson have produced ideas that will be copied in the future. Theirs is a kind of comfortable and acceptable interior design with an ironic sense of history but without the emphasis on sentimentality that is traditionally associated with Kitsch. We are thus liberated from much of what is snobbishly called good taste.

In this LA house Korpinen and Erickson employ Kitsch in an original way. Respectable furniture and cult objects are mixed with risqué shapes, colours and textures to stir up questions about taste: what is good, comfortable, vulgar or cutting edge? Certainly taste used as a cultural weapon is unpleasant, but conversely it is necessary for self-identity and pleasure.

VENTURING INTO THE SIXTIES
AND SEVENTIES

The sixties provided a self-conscious break with the past. Open-plan living has its draw-backs, however. How were we to deal with an increase in noise levels, lack of privacy and the shortage of wall space against which to place furniture? But the bonus of the liberating size and openness of the rooms, the generous windows and increased light levels and the wider opportunity for self-expression was great.

Loved or loathed, rejected or just plain bemusing, the impact of cultural change in the sixties was massive. Social attitudes altered, and technology moved on. There was a desperate desire to sweep away the cobwebs of war. Old or 'straight' attitudes were taboo, which meant that there was a real need to be and feel modern. This was necessary for everyone, not only for those doing a creative job, such as designers, artists and musicians, but also for people in the academic world, industry and the professions. Looking back on it from the safety of a 30-year gap, it seems the participants were in something of a rush for change. That conventions were broken was good. But how far do you dismantle traditions built up over a long period of time? Is it wise to ignore history and all established practice?

All sorts of barriers did need to be broken down – social and political, artistic and ethical – but, with hindsight, respect for the past also took an unnecessary nosedive. The pendulum has swung back since, for example in the conservation of old buildings, but not until the late seventies, by which time a lot of damage had been done. The new needs to be tempered by the old and vice versa. Optimism is the brother of invention, and without it innovation cannot flourish. But unless there is an historical context, the good gets banished and critical faculties are of little use.

The spirit of optimism, of adventure and pursuit of the new is what the sixties at its best had to offer. In *The Shock of the New* (1991), Robert Hughes' erudite and revealing book, he reveals the driving forces behind twentieth-century modern art as being the search for the new. The vigour of this stimulus finally reached the public realm by the sixties and materialized in popular art and music, fashion and product design as well as in the furnishing of our homes. Modern art at the beginning of the sixties was still a preserve of the élite, ready and waiting for popularization by the newly unleashed forces of mass communication. It filtered down quickly to mass-market manufacturers and middle-brow culture-pedlars, the world of design included. It was the intellectual umbrella under which to take cover. It was a chance to make images that could belong unquestionably to the time. How comfortable and enduring they were is another question.

BELOW
This luxurious open-plan English apartment eschews modular units to achieve a balance through its understatement and simplicity. The metal tubular furniture, low glass and metal coffee table and striking globe-shaped, suspended light are all quintessential to the era. The presence of books always adds a civilizing element to any interior.

OPPOSITE
Late sixties' London apartment, using colour and playing games with scale (the oversized armchairs around the fireplace). The room evokes an atmosphere of comfortable bonhomie that belies any slavish following of a decorative style. Here is the essentially controlled lack of clutter that is in keeping with the times. There was a more restrained use of colour as the seventies progressed.

The brave new materials were plastics, including vinyl, polyester, polypropylene, formica, nylon and latex, most of which are still used but in modified form. They did not perform to expectations and had poor breathing properties, making them feel unpleasant and clammy next to the skin; they reflected light in a dull way, and their pigments were damaged by sunlight; they wore badly – particularly formica – and when used in large quantities had an unremitting consistency that makes natural materials such as wood, cotton and stone appear to have subtle and humane variations, with a more lively countenance as well as being eminently touchable.

The new emphasis for furniture in the home was an all-out enthusiasm for systems or modular units. This fitted in well with the reductionist aesthetic of Modernism, where the ghosts of Mondrian lingered; it suited manufacturers because it could increase the repetitiveness of the manufacturing process and make ordering and selling more straightforward.

Standardization was the hidden battle cry of the profit-seeking manufacturers. For the designers it was elegance or minimalism; but in some respects this simplicity ended up transferring our innate desire for comfort into other spheres, such as excessively bright colours on walls and extravagantly geometric patterns in carpets, curtains and wallpapers. In furniture exotic veneers or colours compensated for the new simplicity; upholstered furniture, by rejecting traditional construction techniques and switching to foam or latex filling, took on a rather rigid appearance and, with the assistance of the economic and ubiquitous spiky legs, often set at angles, created a formidable appearance.

The overall look of a dedicated contemporary sixties' house does give the impression of efficiency, order and control, especially when contrasted with our interiors in the mid-nineties. Here comfort, mixed styles of furniture and the obvious enjoyment of the blend of historical and contemporary objects, along with more clutter, makes for a more relaxed atmosphere. Though sixties' interiors might seem enviably clear of bric-à-brac from the past, is this something that is really sustainable for a humane and unselfconscious way of life? Art objects, careful selection of 'icons' from our own and our families' past are part of our nesting instinct. But this must be balanced with open space that allows for the practical activities that we rely on a house to provide. A clear-out never does any harm, however, and perhaps the sixties filled that particular role quite well. But, preparing the way for the eighties, it left behind some interesting clutter. Thirty years in our speeded-up world equals history, and, sixties' bric-à-brac is now looked upon with nostalgia as it is long enough ago to seem part of our past. The sixties has become a 'style' in its own right.

Looking at some of the objects and buildings left behind I feel they were trying much too hard to establish their own identity as a generation. The damage done to old buildings was considerable, and there was a lack of respect of the handmade and for traditional elements of ornament and decoration, a denial of history. Looking back on it from a safe distance we can see the excitement of its revolutionary confidence because it is tempered by time and the assumed superiority of the present.

COUNTRY LIFE REVISITED

One design theme constantly revisited is the Country style, because of its back-to-nature appeal. In it the charms of the countryside are there for us all to see, acting as a safety valve when the pressures of urban life become too great or when the stresses of life in general drive us to seek sanctuary. The concept of a rural existence implies communing with nature, peacefulness and open landscape. Country life in the past certainly wasn't any easier than life in town, but its fantasy image remains strong. It is conceived as an honest, hard-working way of life; where all activity was somehow wholesome and any livelihood well earned.

Farmhouses, cottages and rural dwellings were simply and stoutly furnished, and the no-nonsense attitude towards the design of country furniture, fabrics, household equipment and tools, utensils of all sorts, is perceived as economical, robust and without unnecessary decoration. This rural idyll manifests a puritanical ethos, where excess is eschewed. According to Protestant teachings, those who do not squander are morally pure, so will be looked after by God. Arrival in heaven is assured.

ABOVE

The appeal of rural life forms the palette of materials and variety of construction methods prevalent in the popular image of country kitchens. Shown here is a plate rack made in blacksmith's iron and oiled hardwoods taken from the Sociable Kitchen (pages 89–91). Here there is an implied sense of continuity, a link with the past that is practical in the present and aesthetically pleasing.

RIGHT

In this converted Cornish barn the continued enjoyment of the original construction is evident in the rough-hewn beams and uneven walls, in the handmade furniture – by British designer Alan Brown – and the textured floor rug. All these contribute to pleasurable feelings we gain from the well-worn and the familiar, which is so integral to the idea of comfort.

As comforting as all this is, I think there is more to it than that. Rural life suggests self-reliance and a chance for independent survival, neither exploiting other people nor exploited by them. It ultimately goes back to a slightly idealized version of peasant life, where, like the modern taste for peasant cookery with its rough-and-ready seasonal ingredients, the best was made out of the materials at hand. Making do and improvizing with locally available materials, constructed with no pandering to aesthetics, has work-a-day charm that is often visible in so-called country-made objects, tools and furniture.

One book that evokes this rural reality strongly for me is *Lark Rise to Candleford* by Flora Thompson. Originally published in 1939, Thompson paints a portrait of a fast-disappearing England of peasants, yeomen and craftsmen. Of folk who lived with cheerful courage, enjoying the rare pleasures that marked their self-sufficient world of work and poverty. In a quote from the excellent introduction by H. J. Massingham: 'Farm and workshop both were husbanded with responsible stewardship.... Home as the centre alike of the family and of industry, and the nucleus of neighbourliness, was the ruling concept of both. One character, Uncle Tom, displays personal integrity, a pride in his work and a virile personality with the intent of revealing good living and the good life as an historical unity of the older England.'

Massingham goes on, 'Another character "Old Sally", who is so closely identified with her house and furniture, its two-feet thick walls making a snuggery for her gateleg table, the dresser with its pewter and willow pattern ware and the grandfather's clock, is an example of self-supporting peasant England, its bedrock.' The atmosphere of her house is thoroughly practical, hardworking, thinly furnished but humane and, if only just comfortable, certainly comforting. Not surprisingly *Lark Rise to Candleford* became a cult book in the seventies, 30 years after its initial publication.

The mystery of ancient woodland, the beauty of the landscape with its endless variety and the effects of changing seasons, as well as a timeless continuity summon up a powerful and appealing set of images for the pastoral way of life. How can they be resisted, especially when magazines and newspapers constantly devote themselves to rural charms, and designers and artists draw inspiration from them? They cannot. But, does their evocation need to be bogus? No, quite the reverse.

The Country style will always be with us as a focus for a more relaxed way of designing homes. It is in some ways anti-style, perpetuating the idea that anything goes together; just less planned or designed, but using simpler, more robust furniture, finishes and down-to-earth furnishings. The recent trend for converting barns and lofts shows how easily the Country style adapts to both large and small spaces and suits the tastes of a cultivated aesthetic. The 'Long Island' style, despite its nautical flavour, is essentially derived from the juxtaposition of heightened Country-style finishes and artefacts. Only the preponderance of the colour blue and some seascape paraphernalia gives it a coastal tang. At its core is still the use of natural materials and a no-nonsense simplicity.

The harder, less glamorous, aspects of rural life in late nineteenth-century Britain are evoked in ths painting by George Smith Musing on the Future *(1874). Rough walls, worn floor tiles, make-do curtains, a scrubbed table-top and wooden chairs remind one of the harsher realities of country life in the nineteenth century. Nevertheless, the image of this cottage kitchen/parlour is a fine example of a hardworking room for all the family, and one that is still invoked, albeit in a refined form, over a century later.*

There is an attempt, at times, by all of us to live more honestly and with greater truth. The Arts and Crafts movement stemmed from this and is manifest in the late twentieth century by the revival of Mission-style furniture in the United States; in the UK this is seen in the continuing plethora of Country-style inspired fashions, from fabrics, kitchens and furniture to clothes. It is a mawkish look when too nostalgic but can be used intelligently and without sentimentality. In modern Scandinavian design or in imported ethnic or peasant-made items, where tradition has not been fiddled with too much, it is thoroughly usable and appropriate for our hardworking lives. There is a special quality about handmade objects, whether primitive or just traditional. The difference is still tangible between the machine-made and hand-executed, though with many honourable exceptions. The Sussex trug, Shaker craftware and handmade flower pots spring to mind as obvious examples. All evoke the spirit of skill and hard work, and, in keeping with the thesis of this book, also perform well and give pleasure.

So, too, do well designed objects that have been partially or even largely made by machines, but not quite in the same way. Their advantage is more

A modern adaptation of the Country look, 'Shabby Chic'. Simple furnishings, loose-fitting sofa covers, a lack of precious antiques and a staircase descending in the corner are all reminiscent of old parlours and cottage kitchens.

to do with being well engineered, carefully thought through and expertly carried out than the subtler pleasures found in the handmade, where too much perfection can be counterproductive. Visible evidence of the stroke of the craftsman's hand, or flaws in the weaver's weft showing hand construction, indicate shades of humanity that machine-made goods do not have. The choice has to be made between them, for they are different genres, and both have their individual and satisfactory qualities.

Honesty, integrity, simplicity, all attributes first expressed by the Arts and Crafts movement, live on in their furniture and buildings. Inextricably associated with traditional, untainted country life, these are the qualities that I have tried to express in this narrow kitchen.

HISTORICAL
INFLUENCES
ON THE
HARDWORKING
HOUSE

The Georgian period accommodated both robust country furniture and the high-class elegance appropriate for grander spaces, as can be seen in the design of these chairs at Silas Deane House (1766), which are a kind of robust country Chippendale pattern.

Introduction

OPPOSITE
Panelled, early seventeenth-century dining room in a sixteenth-century Tudor manor in Buckinghamshire, Dorney Court.

BELOW
Sturdy geometry, appropriate materials and decorative sensibilities link this twelfth-century kitchen made for me by Jonathan Morriss.

IMPLICIT in the thesis that I have been developing so far is the idea of a humane and comfortable shell in which a civilized life is possible. What underpins this is an empirically developed set of practical ideas of what is worth handing on to the next generation. In each historical period and each European culture in which these practical and technological developments happened they were judged in the mental climate of their times. They were tested and approved and allowed to go forward. In the section that follows, I have selected six commonly identifiable periods or movements that provide the best historical contributions to the idea of the Hardworking House.

The Georgian Legacy

Fᴇw epochs have left such a lasting impact on Western taste and culture as the Georgian period (1714–1830) in Britain. Its legacy was awesome. Its continual popularity is worth understanding. Designers and architects still use it as a kind of benchmark, where good taste, refinement, simplicity and a sense of order come together. During the eighteenth century so many aspects of cultural life converged, from music, art, scientific ideas and literature to philosophy, creating a sense of greatness and stability. That Georgian was modern in its day, too, is worth remembering; likewise its avoidance of the sentimentality seen in much nineteenth-century Victorian culture. Georgian style was a broad church of taste, able to incorporate a range of influences from Gothic, Dutch and Chinese to the simple Country-style furniture-making traditions. If we accept that this was a period of the culmination of good taste, where the cultural forces of the day somehow created a unique confluence of perfection, how did it come about?

Georgian life, depicted here in The Dutton Family *by eighteenth-century painter Johann Zoffany, still acts now as a kind of benchmark where good taste is concerned. Refinement of so many aspects of civilized life came together at this time, particularly in the fields of design, architecture, painting, music and literature. Note the vibrant colour of the walls as a backdrop to such a polished era.*

G. M. Trevelyan in *An Illustrated English Social History* (vol. 2, 1952) offers the kind of traditional explanation that we like to hear. He says that 'taste had not yet been vitiated by too much machine production. Both the maker and the purchaser of goods still thought in terms of handicraft. The artist and the manufacturer were not yet divided poles asunder.... Life and art were still human, not mechanical, and quality counted far more than quantity.' He claims that the aristocracy still set the tone of bourgeois taste, and that their leaders were not harassed by the perpetual itch to make money. This aristocratic atmosphere was much more conducive to good taste than any bourgeois, democratic or totalitarian regimes that occurred in either subsequent periods in Europe or America.

Trevelyan goes on to say that, as patrons of culture, the English aristocracy of the time functioned better than the monarchy. 'The English Royal court circumscribed their interest to the music of Handel. Fine in itself, but limited. The aristocracy, however, had not one centre but hundreds, scattered over the country in gentlemen's estates, each a focus of learning in miniature that made up for the decay at the official universities.'

My own explanation for the success of the Georgian aesthetic was that it had extraordinarily versatile yet disciplined qualities. Derived from classical roots, where highly developed theories on proportion gave guidelines on scale, detail and aesthetic in good manners, it had travelled via the Italian Renaissance, which added useful features and suitably tamed the style for domestic architecture. Georgian England managed to strip it down further to meet the pragmatic demands of the small, medium and large house. The new commercial classes created by the Industrial Revolution in the late-eighteenth and early-nineteenth century employed it for city terraces and the new urban squares. It could travel up and down the size scale, from house fronts to the minutiae of cornice mouldings.

Leading furniture designers and architects made pattern books that disseminated a by now thoroughly adaptable aesthetic, suitable not only for rough country furniture but also for highly sophisticated, revered and carved mantlepieces and gilded furniture for the nation's stately homes and the first British Empire. A wonderful vocabulary of details emerged, demonstrating unique ways of creating things ie door panels, raised mouldings, carved club feet, door entablatures, friezes, fabric designs, china and cutlery, and many other key elements that make up the designer's or maker's operational language. They were kept elegant and well mannered and, unlike their Victorian counterparts, without ostentation, sentimentality or heaviness.

By using pattern books craftsmen employed designs that were well thought out and did not make inappropriate efforts to be original, wacky or overly ambitious. Self-expression took place within a given set of values, but I don't think we could criticize the Georgian period as being an era that lacked originality. A sense of decorum, of good sense, grace and beauty reflected the spirit of the age. This should send a sombre note of warning to us designers and house makers of today.

The Georgian influence is still felt keenly today, visible here in this example from my own design. This games table, where the classic lines and simple elegance were appropriate, could not unintentionally escape Georgian references.

THE GEORGIAN MANOR HOUSE

Houses are built to fit the social and practical needs of their time. Georgian houses reflect the spirit of the age so clearly, and as the era was such a civilized, successful and progressive one, this makes it an enjoyable historical period to study. Some of the most pleasurable and best sources of references to the age are English novelist Jane Austen's works. Even the title of her novel *Sense and Sensibility* (1811) gives us clues to key qualities of the period. Good sense, moderation, progress and humour were considered vital virtues and gave rise to social ones, such as benevolence, prudence, honesty and tolerance. In David Cecil's wonderful *A Portrait of Jane Austen* (1978) he says, 'Its clear breezy climate of good sense and self-confidence made it an age in which humour flourished.' This allowed humour to act as a check on extremism of all kinds. 'Its talk was racy as well as polished,' he continues. 'It could enjoy eccentrics if they were entertaining; it forgave Johnson his uncouthness for the sake of his wit and his wisdom. Like its houses and its chairs and its teacups . . . [it] managed to be at the same time both sensible and stylish.'

The idea of the importance of good taste probably emerged more than ever then as a necessary social grace. Taste, David Cecil says, implied learning and discrimination. The man of sense was a man of taste, for it was civilized and realistic. It demonstrated education in the classical arts, where scholarship and elevation of thought were put above self-interest. The bigger picture of national interest, sound morality or an informed global perspective was the enlightened overview. This mental climate produced a thoroughly modern and vigorous set of values that affected all aspects of architecture, furniture and home furnishings.

The Georgian house must have shocked many of the older generation by its novelty. Its tall, well-proportioned rooms, sash windows with symmetrical, flat façades and a reductionist but clearly 'designed' aesthetic were a determined break with Tudor, Stuart or vernacular predecessors. Crisp joinery detailing, panelling, elegant plasterwork and fine moulding were its hallmark. It provided architectural manners that were so different from previous sensibilities, whether the rough-cut, heavy timber beams, inglenook fireplaces, the small and cramped rooms of older farmhouses or, on a larger scale, the enormous and chilly multi-purpose public rooms of grander houses. In the Georgian manor house the sense of privacy was much improved. The number of rooms was increased with dedicated uses, dividing the house into distinct private and public spaces. Some people must have thought the Georgian manor house uncomfortable and lacking in cosiness, but with the rise of both the sophistication and range of trades and skills that was to be expected; it just needed to become familiar.

The Georgian style was a different aesthetic. The arrival of upholstery techniques from France in the early seventeenth century, the swelling volume of trade that brought rugs from the Orient, the increase in the number of cabinet-makers and their skills and the rise in use of 'design' books, made possible

A new sense of fineness in the detailing of interiors became apparent in the Georgian period. Decorative plasterwork and wooden and stone carving recreated classical motifs in a recognizable formula of its own, as shown here in this chimneypiece, inset with scagliola plaques in imitation of Florentine hardstone mosaic, in the Tapestry Room of Robert Adam's design at Osterley Park.

through development of the printing trades, provide evidence of how and why domestic life was enhanced. Social intercourse and private life were each beginning to be valued more highly, and the greater influence of women enhanced feminine values, with an improvement in manners and an appreciation of 'genteel' behaviour that allowed women's influence to grow more powerful. This affected social customs, percolating through to domestic architecture, with the desire for more graceful furniture and less harsh interiors. Drawing rooms, in particular, were furnished in refined materials, with lightweight, elegant chairs and rugs; gone were heavy furniture, inglenook fireplaces and rough pottery. More than in any previous age there was delicate china, finely carved and upholstered chairs, elegant silverware and other tea-making equipment, from sugar-tongs to tea-caddies.

A typical British West Country manor house, The Lodge, from the late Georgian period. With its good manners and elegant ease of adaptation, it is hardly surprising that the Georgian style became the first truly international style. Even today the majority of new houses in the United States continue to be built within its language.

The Shaker Contribution

For a religious movement to leave behind such a massive impact on the world of design and craft is unique. Without doubt the Shakers' skills in both these areas were exceptional. In part this may have come about because the sect required celibacy. Without children to support, without individual family life, the focus of the men and women was on their work, or duties, which had to be carried out fastidiously. At no time did they consciously set out to develop a design style or to innovate except on a technical level. They worked within the aesthetic milieu of the time, and that was clearly the Georgian style.

In 1758 religious mystic 'Mother' Ann Lee, an English woman raised in the slums of Manchester, joined the Shaking Quakers or Shakers, who saw in her the second coming of Christ. She emigrated to New England in 1774 with eight other Shakers, after her four children had died, and she had been imprisoned for street preaching. In 1776 she founded the parent Shaker settlement there. After a religious revival swept through New England, a Baptist minister heard Lee preaching and persuaded his congregation to follow her. Although Lee died in 1781, the Shaker movement flourished, and by 1840 there were 6000 brothers and sisters.

The sect had strong internal governing laws; for example, in 1845 they passed an edict in which 'Beadings, mouldings and cornices, which are merely for fancy, may not be made by believers'. The Shakers were clearly concerned that their inner beliefs should be reflected in the austerity and simplicity of their built environment. According to June Sprigg and David Larkin in their elegant book, *Shaker Life, Work and Art* (1987), art for its own sake was not acceptable because of its uselessness. A utilitarian approach, appropriate to the pioneering spirit, is obvious in all the Shaker artefacts. But it is not an explanation in itself. There was a sense of religious fervour centred around simplicity, considered next to Godliness, which, combined with the purging of excess and the banishment of emotional attachment to objects, helped the Shakers achieve, with much technical skill, a refinement of contemporary design that was the minimalist aesthetic of its time.

Shaker designs for furniture to this day possess the required monastic austerity that is particularly associated with an ultra-modernist aesthetic. The fineness of the craftsmanship is ever present and there is a constant reminder of how much pleasure there can be in a simple object, so beautifully made that it is almost poetic. From a more practical point of view one of the reasons for the continued popularity of Shaker furniture is its varied and eye-catching ideas for storage. The picture rail with pegs for hanging chairs, boxes, clothes and so on, the multi-drawer cabinet, copious built-in storage features and chests of drawers and useful and intriguing containers of all kinds to suit the needs of a modern house.

RIGHT
A recently designed, freestanding wooden stove by Justin Meath Baker, who works with Christopher Nevile, encapsulates Shaker simplicity and reflects its continuing appeal in the modern tradition. The use of painted, panelled woodwork, function of the dado rail as a kitchen-pan, hanging storage area and simple, uncluttered function at peace with form is at one with the Shaker aesthetic, attractive in our some-times manic modern world.

BELOW
The monastic austerity in Shaker designs appeals to a certain desire in us all for a simple life shorn of unnecessary clutter yet accommo-dating the pleasure of the carefully thought-out and the well made. We express our inner lives in our external environment and in our interiors. The Shakers did so in a very determined, noticeable way. Many people respond to that.

One enjoyable aspect of Shaker furniture is that its quiet and simple lines enable its design to fit well into a wide range of interiors. This asset is multi-plied even more by the variety of uses to which its storage furniture can be put. As I discuss in the following section on the Arts and Crafts, there is an inevitable need for mankind to express themselves spiritually through work and through craftsmanship. This is more discernible in Shaker design than in any other style, group or movement. Furnishing our homes is no different. Although we no longer have visible household gods, like the Romans, or statues of Buddha, as they do in some Eastern cultures, we still express evidence of our inner life in our personal surroundings. One basic way we demonstrate this is through well-made and simply designed objects. Another manifestation is a sense of order and peace in the avoidance of too much clut-ter (William Morris' edict: 'Surround yourself only with what is beautiful or useful' comes to mind). This is all implicit in the Shaker legacy and may well explain the enduring popularity of Shaker design and craftsmanship.

The Early Colonial Home

THE first settlers arrived on the eastern seaboard of America from English rural communities, and most were barely educated, simple folk with artisan and farming skills. With them they brought all their ideas of comfort, which are reflected in their building methods. Their oak timber-frame houses were based on a two-room central-chimney plan. A kitchen was added later as a lean-to, and so family life took place in a multi-functional parlour. The adults slept downstairs, and upstairs was used for storage. By the eighteenth century, in New England, this plan was expanded to four downstairs rooms from a central hall, similar to the well-known 'salt-box' configuration; the influence of the Georgian period started to be apparent. Symmetrical façades, higher ceilings, more spacious rooms – and more of them – panelling or fine plaster mouldings to cover beams and walls, all contained within a generally more sophisticated, controlled sense of design.

There was a wider availability of chinaware, high-quality cabinetmakers' furniture and fine materials, of precious upholstered furniture, glass and silverware. This stemmed not only from the increasing wealth of the colony but also from improved production techniques in England, where the

Silas Deane House (1766), Westerfield, Connecticut. The hardworking nature of this New England kitchen is appealing in the effective use of its materials – mostly wood, using wide boads – and its uncluttered, well-lit design.

Industrial Revolution had begun in the late-eighteenth and early-nineteenth century. The first American design pattern books by Asher Benjamin appeared in *Country Builders' Assistant* (1797) and the *American Builders' Companion* (1806). The early days of mere survival gave way to the more civilizing opportunities that accompany an increase in resources. The beginnings of an indigenous American design culture, polyglot in origin, created a freer interpretation of the Georgian vocabulary of form found in the English pattern books and traditions of the time.

The influence of other settlers' traditions, particularly from Germany, Holland and Scandinavia, added extra richness and originality. Mostly this produced more adventurous and varied results, but at times the divergence from the classic form makes the (usually) English version look more restrained. It is nearly always possible to tell whether furniture was English made or colonial in origin. Both styles have distinctive characteristics; sometimes obvious features or the type of work is revealing. In any case, the furniture that sprang from the roots of the New World culture shows the incredible patience and determination of the people who made it. Certainly woodworking skills were highly sought-after in the Colony. Wendell Garrett's beautiful and well-researched book, *American Colonial* (1995), is a *tour de force*, and he demonstrates, with pictures and in his text, just how rich this period was in terms of its design and craftsmanship.

The Georgian style was so flexible that it was capable of being 'all things to all people'. Here it is austere, but comfortable, and thus well suited to the dominant Protestant ethics of New England.

LEFT
In this main bedroom at Gunston Hall, clearly designed for a wealthier clientele, the comfort level increases along with the degree of opulence.

The Georgian aesthetic influence lasted up to the 1840s, until new-fangled Victorian tastes made their presence felt. The enthusiasm for simple, under-stated elegance diminished and was replaced by an urge for more ostentation, expressed in more ornament, heavier construction and an explosion of retro-stylistic reference, among them Neo-Egyptian, Neo-Gothic, Neo-classical and Neo-Tudor. New technology was dressed up in old clothes to disguise innovation. Railway trains looked like horse-drawn carriages and gas lamps like glorified candlesticks. Everywhere there was a slight discomfort with advancing technology. There is a feeling that the Georgian aesthetic was more at ease with itself, however. Certainly its enduring popularity is evident, particularly in the USA, where many new houses are still built in a deter-minedly Georgian Colonial style. Do these show modern improvements on the Georgian style? Clearly not much on the outside – perhaps more in the interiors. The Georgian style endures well; its appeal to comfort, elegance and proportion is an all-embracing language that remains strongly coherent in western taste values.

ABOVE RIGHT
Over time the design and manu-facture of Georgian furniture and silverware in the colony became extremely sophisticated. Only the china illustrated on this table, seen here displayed in the north-east chamber of Joseph Webb House (1752), Westerfield, Connecticut, would have been imported from England. The slightly simpler, more upright lines of the tripod table give it away as colonial-made.

The Arts and Crafts House:
Integration of Design, Inside and Out

ARCHITECTURAL WORK

Although there was no manifesto as such, Arts and Crafts architects were strongly driven by an ideology based on a belief that the experience of fabricating (and using) artefacts, buildings and furniture should be life enhancing. They wished to side-step the unseemly effects of the Industrial Revolution, which they abhorred. They were also pioneers for upgrading the role of design, wishing to bring together the making and the thinking process. The Modern Movement emphasized standardization as an important part of this evolution, accepting the Industrial Revolution as a *fait accompli*. Peter Davey in his thorough book, *Arts and Crafts Architecture* (1995), more or less comes to the conclusion that it was the last great period where individuality of expression was emphasized, the role of design being important in this way.

William Morris, a leading figure of the Arts and Crafts movement in the latter half of the nineteenth century, was an English designer and decorator, a craftsman and writer of extraordinary talent. His designs for wallpaper and furniture are his most famous legacy. He was strongly influenced by John Ruskin, the pre-eminent architectural critic of the nineteenth century, who set out to prove that Gothic, as the product of free craftsmen, was the true style for Protestants. In *The Lamp of Truth* he claimed that all cast and machine work was bad and set out three rules, known as principles of savageness, which Arts and Crafts architects should follow. In summarized form these were: do not make anything in which invention (or design, I wonder?) has no share; do not demand exact finishes, unless needed for a practical reason; no imitation or copying. Gothic architecture was the only rational architecture because it was flexible, not obsessed with symmetry. If Gothic architects, he said, wanted 'windows they opened one, a room they added one' or indeed anything else. This produced an architectural style that could be described as picturesque. Arts and Crafts architects regarded this as a virtue.

The Red House at Upton in Kent shows this 'changefulness', which was based on Ruskin's idea of savageness and designed by British architect and designer Philip Webb in 1859 for Morris after he married. The interior was a collaboration and included murals by the Pre-Raphaelites Edward Burne-Jones and Dante Gabriel Rossetti, as well as furniture by Morris. Webb's work was delicate, well mannered and less extreme than other Arts and Crafts architects. He designed a number of country houses, among which Clouds at East Knoyle in Wiltshire in the 1880s and Standen near East Grinstead in Sussex in the 1890s are his most celebrated. He developed a real love of building methods and helped to found the Society for Protection of Ancient Buildings,

William and Jane Morris' first house, known as the Red House (1859) at Upton in Kent. It was designed by friend and associate Philip Webb. The interior was a collaboration and includes murals by the Pre-Raphaelites. This view shows their early Gothic instincts, playful and pleasantly restrained.

which he turned into 'a school of practical building with all the whims which we usually call design left out'. 'Over-design', or unnecessary clutter, was a real issue then, like it is today. Conservation was a relatively new idea, and certainly the Society was the first professional body to nurture and develop it. An important part of Arts and Crafts philosophy was to acknowledge past techniques of building.

The drawing room at Standen shows a more domesticated version of Arts and Crafts at work. Its post-Victorian modernity is evident in the use of light, space and simplified forms for furniture and joinery work.

Webb's more prodigious contemporary, the British architect and designer Richard Norman Shaw, developed English Arts and Crafts into a more adventurous, pluralistic phase. A whole range of new styles was adopted as he saw fit, in particular the Queen Anne look for his London commissions and Old English, mostly Tudor in character, for his substantial country houses. Bedford Park (1878) was a celebrated prototype for a new garden suburb in Chiswick, London, the progenitor of the Garden City movement. Solid, upright and airy, the houses in Bedford Park were modern, relatively free of eclectic mannerisms and comfortable as well as extremely popular. In 1884 Norman Shaw also designed a highly accomplished house for the English artist Kate Greenaway in Hampstead, London. It sits comfortably between the nineteenth- and twentieth-century taste values, addressing sensitivities of both the old and the new. Recent 'developers' vernacular' of the 1980s in the United States and Britain could learn from it with their crass attempts at Tudor revival. It is one of those houses that is genuinely transitional in design. It could be classified as late Edwardian or almost early thirties' vernacular, despite being designed in 1884.

Another house ahead of its time was The Barn (1896) in Exmouth, designed by E. P. Prior. He took the favoured long-plan of Arts and Crafts architects – one room deep plus corridor – and broke it in half to angle it with the newly important entrance hall. This acted as a pivot, creating the so-called butterfly-plan, which enabled maximum exposure to one aspect – in this case the sea – and allowed greater penetration of light into the major rooms. Externally the origin and witty insertion of linear groups of giant pebbles into the stonework created a non-designable element that gave clear evidence of the craftsman's input. This textural surprise adds a sense of fun and spontaneity.

The entrance hall was regarded by many Arts and Crafts architects as a room not just for reception or circulation but also, in the medieval sense, as a place for assembly around a fire in the evening. Another leading English domestic architect and designer, Charles Francis Annesley Voysey, designed entrance halls with great care, backing them up with substantial and welcoming porches. His entrance porches had inner seats, side windows and wide doors, and the porch at Vodin, near Woking, is a particularly enchanting example. Voysey's houses have often exaggerated details, such as giant roofs, cornices and wide doors, with moustaches above the circular front doors as well as other fun elements. By all accounts, though, he was quite a sombre man, and his designs – like those of many Arts and Crafts architects – were austere in the interior. He designed some of the most confident and individual houses of the time, including one for the English writer H. G. Wells, who considered Voysey's work as modern in outlook and lacking in pomposity.

There are many other important architects who come in the category of Arts and Crafts and who I have left out. But three more of them deserve mention: Edwin Lutyens, the foremost English architect during the first three decades of the twentieth century; the ubiquitous North American Frank Lloyd Wright – sometimes described as 'the most influential architect

of his time' and also considered a Modernist; and greatest of all, loved for his individuality and sheer inventiveness, Charles Rennie Mackintosh. A Scottish architect and designer, Mackintosh only built two houses and a few interiors, as well as his famous Glasgow School of Art (1897–9) and its library block and other extensions (1907–9). No study is complete without assessing his contribution. His reputation has swollen to immense proportions, especially since the Second World War, although his work was a fundamental element of Art Nouveau and was widely recognized in Germany and Austria early on.

Mackintosh integrated architecture, furniture and interior design. His furniture, in particular, made strong statements, but his skill as a painter was such that he could easily realize a wide range of decorative details, including designs for wallpaper, plasterwork, stained glass and upholstery fabric. The latter, with their swirling shapes, helped provide the Arts and Crafts and Art Nouveau movements with a rich variety of motifs and ornament. In addition Mackintosh firmly established the influence of the Japanese aesthetic as a major source for the subsequent modernistic philosophy. Quiet, strong lines,

Hillsborough House (1902–3), near Glasgow, designed by Charles Rennie Mackintosh. He integrated architecture, interior and furniture design with immense determination. His originality, along with Japanese influence, had a great impact on design in Western cultures later on in the century.

restraint of material, minimal but clean decorative details, emphasis on harmony and the value of empty space were his hallmarks. These were ideas at odds with Edwardian and late-Victorian taste. His furniture, going beyond Arts and Crafts' obsession with craftsmanship, pushes the use of wood to its limit, employing it more to make a visual impact with its design than for its natural texture, and novel enamel-painted finishes are used to create the illusion of modernity. Exploitation of joints and junctions show an extraordinarily inventive mind at work. Mackintosh was a rare combination of artist and architect, designer and decorator all rolled into one. He never compromised his integrity or pandered to contemporary taste, unlike others, such as Lutyens, who were less concerned with self-expression and more concerned with pragmatism.

By the time Edwin Lutyens' career fully blossomed he had turned to classicism, but his earlier period of country-house building, which most rate more highly, was carried out within the Arts and Crafts' aesthetic. Strongly influenced by Voysey, and working with Gertrude Jekyll, the garden designer and horticulturalist, he showed a flexible and inventive mind at work.

The Charles Rennie Mackintosh bedroom at Derngate (1915–17) in Northampton demonstrated a supreme control in the application of his design aesthetic across the spectrum of furniture, fabric design and lighting. He was a rare combination of artist, interior and furniture designer and serves as a role model for many architects today – albeit ambitious and perhaps unsuitably overcontrolling in a domestic environment for many people.

Frank Lloyd Wright's own living room at his home, Taliesin (1911), in Spring Green, Wisconsin. In this phase of his work he was loosening his ties with the English Arts and Crafts movement but retained many of its sensibilities: the use of wood, the Japanese influence and enjoyment of craftsmanship. He was involved in the building of Taliesin himself. He went on to design another home and school, Taliesin West, near Phoenix in Arizona, in 1938.

Frank Lloyd Wright, or FLW as he is affectionately known, is the best example of the transitional foot-in-two-camps architect; not that he would have been aware of this – or even cared.

Wright lived to an old age and thus had the chance to work within the architectural milieu of later times, his architecture spanning a 72-year career from the late 1880s to his death in 1959. Born around 1866 (there is some doubt over the exact date), he lived till his nineties and so was able to adapt to the Modern Movement's ideologies in the second phase of his work, after World War Two. His roots, though, were firmly in the Arts and Crafts tradition, and his eccentric lifestyle and flamboyant personality belong more to an earlier period. The excellent biography of him by Brendan Gill, entitled *Many Masks* (1987), provides a fulsome account of his long, rich and racy life.

There is no doubt of an early Arts and Crafts influence. Wright had read Ruskin's *Seven Lamps*, argued for a revival of the Gothic spirit in the mid-West and was a friend of Charles Robert Ashbee, the British architect, designer, silversmith and jeweller who gave talks in Chicago in 1900, as the Arts and Crafts chief philosopher. By this time Wright had begun to evolve his own unique Prairie style.

Frank Lloyd Wright is a transitional architect, moving between styles, showing where Arts and Crafts and Modernism connected. His enthusiasm was for horizontal lines, as in the Robie House (1908–10), Chicago, Japanese influence and open-planning.

The latter wasn't his invention, just an adaptation of a North American tradition whereby the hall in the early New England salt-box houses became used as a sociable room in its own right. Corridors were considered wasteful of valuable space, and the logical progression of doing away with transitional spaces is that every room is used for both circulation and occupation. So why not treat this as a *fait accompli* in the plan? Frank Lloyd Wright also introduced a primitive form of central heating in the Robie House, which finally eliminated the necessity for enclosed spaces around fireplaces and doorways. Sound privacy remained the only main obstacle to open-plan, visual privacy to a lesser extent.

Voysey, with his enthusiasm for 'real' entrance halls, still retained corridors for other rooms because the English had sustained the tradition for them; but Frank Lloyd Wright has been able, because of American traditions, to merge the English customary design of the great central living hall into an all-in-one space that embraced the functions of living room, drawing room, parlour and entrance hall into one. Perhaps American sense of privacy is less cherished, as Peter Davey suggests in *Arts and Crafts Architecture*. Certainly the lack of hedges and open front gardens in most New England houses points to it.

Frank Lloyd Wright's main disagreement with C. R. Ashbee was in his use of machines, which, rather than eschewing, Wright embraced, speaking of 'their wonderful cutting, shaping, smoothing and reinterpreting' capacity. He was clearly ready to accept the major tenet of the Modern Movement when its cultural influence reached him.

ARTS AND CRAFTS INFLUENCE: FURNITURE AND INTERIORS

Unlike many styles or movements, where aesthetics play a primary role, for the Arts and Crafts pioneers the method of manufacture was equal to the design. John Ruskin, its spiritual father, believed that hand labour was a human right and suggested that designer and craftsman should be reunited in a single person 'the workman ought to be thinking and the thinker ought to be working.' British architect, designer, writer and teacher William R. Lethaby, who, along with William Morris, devoted part of his energy to acting as a scribe for the movement, declared in 1968 that 'beauty can only be brought back to common life by our doing common work in an interesting way.' Later, as pointed out by Peter Davey, he refined it to: 'All work of man bears the stamp of the spirit but this stamp is not necessarily ornament.'

Morality, right from the start, played a role. William Morris, the chief prophet of the Arts and Crafts movement, was driven by a strong Utopian

The hall of Melsetter House (1898) in Orkney, Scotland, by William Lethaby. A return to the medieval idea of the hall as the main room in which to gather was a key enthusiasm of Arts and Crafts architects. As one of their chief intellectuals, Lethaby wrote tracts for them. Here austerity and beauty seem too closely linked to each other from a modern-day standpoint.

vision. Social reform played a big part in this. Not only were the aesthetics to be pure, honest and free of superfluous decoration but the way furniture was to be made had also to be life enhancing, using both traditional and local materials. Expressed, hand-made construction joints were important, thereby raising the dignity of labour and craftsmanship to a high status.

But there were problems, for, inevitably, this level of architecture and design was only available to the affluent. This was something that concerned Gustav Stickley of Syracuse, New York State. After visiting Ashbee and Voysey in England, Stickley set up the Gustav Stickley Co., which he enlarged in 1900 to become the Craftsman Workshops. With his magazine, *The Craftsman*, first published in 1901, he combined the Arts and Crafts aesthetic with a judicious use of machine-based activity to make affordable furniture now known as the Mission style. *The Craftsman* proselytized for Arts and Crafts ideals and acted as a pattern book for its readers, employing architects to draw up details of low-cost houses, as well as offering free designs of the furniture. Charles Sumner Greene and Henry Mathew Greene, the famous Californian Arts and Crafts architects and interior designers, used Mission Furniture in their first house. At the Gamble House (1907–9) Greene & Greene have left behind some of the most highly considered and classic examples of architect-designed joinery. The construction ideas are the most sophisticated attempts yet to understand the properties of wood, and to design with and for its qualities in a technical and aesthetic sense. This is Arts and

With its superb woodwork and strong lines, this detail from the staircase understructure at the Gamble House is the ultimate integration of architecture with joinery. The interior planning too is spacious, light and well laid out. The historical references are unusual in being Chinese rather than Japanese, but the intelligence and sureness with which the design is executed makes it a symbol of reverence for many of today's designers.

Crafts working at its best. The historicism, in particular the medievalism, is absent, and even though there is a Chinese aesthetic influence, this doesn't swamp the innovativeness of the whole. Instead it retains the intended simplicity of Arts and Crafts interiors, which were intended to be spartan.

Although I myself find chairs of this period a little uncomfortable and the furniture in general somewhat austere, I cannot deny that there is something attractive about its simplicity, especially after the style obsession of the 1980s. Interestingly, in the 1880s a similar experience was occurring. Victorian ornateness had reached its zenith; sentimentality and the stylistic confusion of endless 'period' revivals – High and Low Gothic, chinoiserie, Neo-classicism, Neo-Rococo, to name but a few – must have left people gasping for a breath of the fresh and spartan Arts and Crafts air. Suddenly walls were unadorned with hectic wallpaper, furniture was more simply made. And, generally, there was less. The Victorians could have done well with the idea of less is more.

Dining-room sideboard, a product possibly of the English designer Harold Stewart Rathbone (1858–1929), at Philip Webb's Standen, complete with blue and white Chinese porcelain. It enjoys the pleasurable ambiguity of being neither a freestanding piece of furniture nor an architectural fitting. The panelling has clearly been designed with a sideboard in mind, with shelves fitted above.

In many ways the late-Victorian interior reflects its occupants' needs to bolster up their lives with imagined experience, through the use of pictures, photographs and bizarre bric-à-brac, as well as providing a degree of comfort in their familiarity. Perhaps it is indicative of the confusion caused by the fast-changing social, political and industrial events of the period. By switching into a pre-industrial, pseudo-medieval world, with craftsmen living honest, rural existences without pollution and ersatz objects (everything was handmade) and without industrial workers toiling away in smog-ridden factory towns, it was possible to create a guilt-free and more enjoyable version of reality. The same applies today. It is pleasant, even necessary, to escape some of the unsatisfactory side-effects of modern-day life – such as traffic, pollution, and poverty – and nowhere is it more vital to do this than in your own home.

There is another association that the Arts and Crafts makes with its pure morality-driven aesthetic – the monastic one. The monk living his quiet and holy life only uses the barest essentials of furniture, while his spiritual life is rich and his soul is content – something we all want, probably more than anything else. Is it any coincidence that the Arts and Crafts' most successful furniture in the United States is called the Mission style? The Shaker legacy and Arts and Crafts movement are two design styles that seem to touch the right chord with many of us because of their semi-religious and moral overtones. They compensate, perhaps, for the collapse in our religious values, and the certainty these can perpetuate. In the West we miss that spiritual conviction, taken for granted in previous centuries.

A Brief History of the Modern House

The human mind has an exceptional capacity for invention and places great importance on expanding its knowledge and seeking out the new. The modern house, as part of the twentieth-century art and design movement described generally as Modernism, represents part of the desire by inventive individuals to be at the cutting-edge, constantly pushing ideas to their limit. The pace of change this century is arguably the fastest of any period in recorded history, and I am only able to look here at the few key houses that represent landmarks in the development of the twentieth-century house.

Modernism has unleashed a tremendous energy and radical approach across the whole spectrum of our artistic imagination. It challenges the relationship between technology and art, mass production and design, architecture and use of space, sculpture and three-dimensional form. It has changed our attitude to self-expression and launched a series of new ideas and movements, such as Constructivism, Cubism, Realism, Surrealism, Abstract Art and Minimalism, to name but a few.

New ideas about the design of the house started in England before the turn of the century with the Arts and Crafts movement, inspired by the ideas of William Morris. This helped to create a climate open to innovation, especially in the United States, Germany and France, where its influence had begun to spread. The British did not take to Modernism in their homes, or in public architecture, which is where its ideas found their earliest appeal. In some respects Modernism's advantages – exploitation of space and penetration of light – enjoy their greatest advantage in warm climates.

Northern zones see the house as offering protection from cold and keeping out the effects of weather. In hot climates the weather needs to be filtered, for example, by using wind to bring air through the building. And verandas can be built as transition rooms that can be used flexibly for activities and in response to temperature change. Ultimately, though, the capacity to experiment is a matter of courage, imagination and open mindedness, not a question of climate.

Individual architects and designers working in their separate countries brought together an overwhelming body of ideas and work. The Austrian architect and theorist Adolf Loos was one of the earliest pioneers with his Steiner House, built in the USA in 1910. It had a flat roof, rectangular windows and no ornament; it was also very plain but, interestingly, of a symmetrical design, unlike later 'modern' houses, where asymmetry was the norm. Fellow architect Frank Lloyd Wright could perhaps be considered the father of the modern house. His early Japanese influence, in common with the Arts and Crafts movement, gave him a passion for clean lines and horizontal planes with an audacious simplicity of form, and his contribution as a transitional architect is discussed earlier. His Prairie houses show all this clearly from around 1886 onward. Oak Park, Chicago (1889–90) is a good example.

Gerrit Thomas Rietveld, the Dutch architect and pioneer of furniture design, was a member of the De Stijl group. He came under Wright's spell, which, combined with the influence of the Dutch painter Piet Mondrian, a fellow member of De Stijl, made him instrumental in breaking the stranglehold that the Arts and Crafts movement had on early Modernism. Starting as an avant-garde furniture-maker, Rietveld's designs for a sideboard and various chairs made an enormous impact. Later on he became the Dutch member of Congrès internationaux d'Architecture moderne (CIAM), the architectural organization formed in 1928 in Switzerland, which held international congresses for the discussion of avant-garde architecture. CIAM's membership included German architect and Bauhaus founder Walter Gropius, the American Eames Bros, German Expressionist Bruno Taut, Dutch architect J. J. P. Oud and the Hungarian-born American architect and designer Marcel Breuer, to name a few.

BELOW
The Schröder House (1924), Utrecht, by Rietveld. An experiment in geometry with unnamed rooms. The first European open-plan house, it epitomizes in architectural terms the De Stijl art movement, with its interest in balanced assymetry.

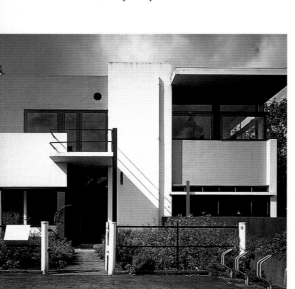

ABOVE RIGHT
Le Corbusier's Villa Savoye (1928–30), Poissy. The ultimate rationalist, fed by his passion for engineering, mathematics and honest use of materials, now a Modernist icon. The house was built as a holiday home for a wealthy patron.

For an exhibition in Berlin in 1924 Rietveld built the Schröder House. According to Daniel Baroni, author of a definitive book on Rietveld, it was the first European open-plan house. More than that, though, it was an experiment in geometry; only in the placing of objects or furniture could the purpose of the space be defined. The traditional idea of a 'room' was absent. Space as understood by De Stijl was infinite and abstract. The first public housing that displayed Modernist notions followed the next year, also in Berlin. Designed by Bruno Taut in the Britz district of Berlin, though not as extreme as Rietveld, the ideas behind its design were radical in terms of a housing project.

Two icons of the modern house, both in France, followed. French architect Charles Edouard Jeanneret, known as Le Corbusier, designed the Villa Savoye (1928–30) at Poissy. It is a triumphalist statement of Modernist architecture, and Le Corbusier emerged as the most influential Modernist architect. He campaigned, wrote a manifesto and developed an ideology for the Modern Movement. Le Corbusier's enthusiasm was for engineering and mathematics,

for non-emotional, highly functional buildings. He was a rationalist, who wanted hardworking architecture. With his undoubted design skills and strong philosophy, Le Corbusier became God to many of the century's architects and a major influence. His megalomaniac tendencies led to ideas that included frighteningly over-planned ideal cities, and, despite his enthusiasm and capacity for poetic expression, his vision did not acknowledge the need we have in our private lives for a humane and comforting living space, but he did make a real contribution to the development of the modern house. He focused us more on the importance of function, performance of materials and the sheer enjoyment of space and light as assets in their own right, with a freedom from the extreme expressions of comfort-psychology. This was seen as sentimentality and a kind of soggy absorption in the clutter of life. My vision of a hardworking house probably stands somewhere in the middle of all this.

The bathroom of the Villa Savoye by Le Corbusier, full of invention, but, looked at with today's sensibility, it is still far too unyielding for domestic life. No one, however, can doubt Le Corbusier's brilliance at conceiving magnificent buildings through the clever manipulation of light and employment of sculptural sensibilities.

OPPOSITE
The interior of the library at the Maison de Verre (1931) by Pierre Chareau. An expression of crafts-manship not philosophy, now much revered. It achieved homo-geneity of light and fluidity of space and was intended to become a blueprint, or model, for artisans to copy. The house is full of inven-tion and obvious enjoyment of craftsmanship. Unfortunately it is not open to the public.

BELOW
Walter Gropius' own house (1938), in Lincoln, Massachusetts, now administered by the American National Trust. It is a sober, rational attempt at restricting the dwelling to a non-emotional configuration of geometric analysis of spatial needs and its expression through a marriage of craftsman-ship and industry.

In 1931 the Maison de Verre by Pierre Chareau, uncelebrated until recently, was completed in Paris. It was an expression of craftsmanship rather than philosophy and was built almost without drawings. It contained much originality and was the first building to use the glass brick. Pierre Chareau wanted the house to be a model made by artisans with a view towards stan-dardization. His basic intentions included freedom of planes, fluidity of space, homogeneity of light and, arguably, the incorporation of services through separate elements. As a cabinetmaker by profession, he had a great love of craftsmanship. One of the reasons the Maison de Verre has become so much loved is because of the visual enjoyment in its sheer mastery of detail that employs design and craftsmanship with such sympathy and finesse. It has the atmosphere of a house that serves its occupants well – that can work hard.

The migration to the USA of many of the leading German architects and members of the influential Bauhaus, the German school of architecture and applied arts, was due to its dissolution by the Nazis in 1933 (they hated the so-called decadence of Modernism). Among them was Walter Gropius, who built a house for himself in Lincoln, Massachusetts, in 1938. Sober, rational and determined by its geometry, it was a Bauhaus version of a New England Colonial home and demonstrated Gropius' interest in the marriage of craft and industry. The house employed industrial materials, including glass bricks, metal windows, lighting equipment and floor and wall finishes. The planning

One of the greatest mentors for Modernist designers was traditional Japanese architecture with its inherently rational and geometric construction, simple lines, use of natural materials and lack of ornament, as shown in this traditional Tea Ceremony Pavilion by Harutaki Ohishi.

General view of the Eames House (1949), Pacific Palisades, California. The application of a geometric grid system was innovative and clever, and its value has not yet been fully exploited. In Eames' hands, it was used with humanity and originality. It is one of the icons of Modernism.

was based on early New England homes around a central hall but with fewer inner walls and using curtains and screens to achieve a greater sense of openness. It adapted traditional Japanese ideas with both American Colonial and the new radical concepts about space of the more extreme, contemporary Modernists. The Lincoln House was both compact and spacious. A clever achievement, it retained enough of a commonality with the traditional idea of the home to be understood by the general public.

John Entenza, editor of the influential *Arts and Architecture,* had declared in 1946 that it was time to stop dreaming and start building, and he proposed a series of case-study houses 'using war-born techniques and materials best suited to the expression of man's life in the modern world'. The climate of optimism released by the end of the Second World War fitted in comfortably with the spirit of Modernism and its yearning to utilize the rediscovered powers of mass production.

Charles and Ray Eames completed their house, Pacific Palisades, in California in 1949. Charles Eames employed a modular steel-grid system, into which he fitted standardized doors, windows and panels, which were painted. The influence of Piet Mondrian is visible, likewise that of the traditional Japanese house, both because of its grid and its quiet aesthetic. Michael Webb in *Architects House Themselves* (1994) provides an excellent summary of its achievements. 'The genius of the house lies in its fusion of Art and Technology, container and contained, the natural and the man made. Nothing is disguised, and there is a simple beauty in the exposed steel frame, ribbed board ceiling, linoleum floor, birch strip rear wall.' The house as a framework for life rather than as its backdrop was how Charles Eames saw it. At the time that was a key part of Modernist philosophy, of doing more with less, being economical, using materials that work well and endure. It is definitely a 'designed' building, but the presence of the designer is not heavily felt – contrary to so many 'designed' houses and interiors of recent years, bristling with over-control and self-conscious detail.

The last architect in this period of great Modernists is Finn Alvar Aalto. He combined his feeling for space and a Modernist's sensibility for light, simplicity and rationality of planning with a singular reverence for craftsmanship and detail. Like many of his compatriots, the culmination of northern winters spent making things to occupy the long dark evenings engendered in him a respect for craftsmanship. Aalto was a great furniture designer, and many of his designs are still in production.

Modernism and the ideas that embody it now span a wide cultural field, so much so that it is the dominant force in twentieth-century aesthetics. But by the late nineties it has come to be severely questioned. Traditional ideas are

reasserting themselves. Is Modernism just another style, a cynic might ask? The response must be a slippery yes and no. Yes, in the sense that it is possible to live, design and operate without using its aesthetic in visible terms (there are plenty of historical and cultural sources from which to choose). But, no if we are making use of contemporary sources for inspiration in interior-design architecture. Modernism is currently undergoing a renewal by absorbing the more humane qualities that will ensure its continued relevance and vitality. But I doubt it will regain the predominance it achieved with the intelligentsia during its heyday. The issue now is surely how to balance the essence of Modernism, its desire for the new, for invention, with the traditional or tried, tested and loved. Perhaps this is the role of 'designing' anyway. The resolving of opposites to create a responsive, practical and rich environment.

An Alvar Aalto house designed for Louis Carré in the early sixties in Bazoches, France. Daring simplicity allied with a great confidence in his aesthetic was achieved partly through tremendous respect and knowledge of craftsmanship and material.

The Japanese House and Culture of Smallness

A traditional Japanese domestic interior at its most appealing. Here there is extreme simplicity of form with an emphasis on the known geometry of the grid system, the tatami *mat, access to garden and lack of visible clutter or furniture. This suits the smaller apartments that most Japanese live in today.*

No study of the modern house is complete without an acknowledgement of the influence of the Japanese. They are the true forebears of 'modern' architecture, who developed a mature aesthetic before Western architects dreamed up the concepts of Modernism. I was led to it by an admiration for both their architecture and the detail and execution of their woodwork.

The modernity of Japanese architecture stems from simplicity of forms, its emphasis on geometry and structure – with an implication of prefabricated parts – its floor-plan based on a rectangular unit (*tatami* mats) and its accent on light, air and utility. There is connection to the garden and nature, and a rejection of pomposity, bolted-on ornament and visual clutter. When Japanese art and culture first made its entrée into the Western world in the 1860s, its impact was immediate and widespread. Exhibitions at leading

museums spread the message in a century hungry for new influence. It offered a refreshing and completely different set of values as well as inspiration to painters, potters, architects and furniture-makers. It was a real breath of fresh air amid the staleness of Victorian sentimentality. Today, we might feel over-exposed to it, just as we are to many overdone cult influences, but there is so much depth to its cultural traditions that they have plenty to offer us if we have time to learn once more. I can only be brief, but I offer here a summary of its basic tenets and some of my own reflections.

At the core of Japanese architecture is their use of asymmetry as a means of setting out buildings, which is opposite to the Western tradition of classical symmetry. Japanese perceptions require a dynamic beauty, where left and right create a sense of balance, movement and surprise. This creates a sort of comfortable tension, based on a triangular geometry rather than, say, a predictable square. Our Arts and Crafts and Gothic traditions are close to this but less influential than 'classical' ideas.

The Japanese view of nature strongly influences their idea of symmetry. They value the uniqueness and predictability of natural forms. For example, they incorporate uncut trees or poles in their natural state with dressed timber, known as *toko-bashira*. If the wood is gnarled or has an unusual shape, this is a

In the Momochi Tarukan Tea Garden, Kyoto, Japan, the lack of furniture, the simplicity of uncluttered space, the connection to garden and the impact of a clearer and geometric structural system offer such a different tradition to the Western idea of home. The central courtyard gives access to nature for all surrounding rooms. The resultant stretched-out planning helps with sound, privacy, light and air movement.

bonus. Because of the adjacent cut and prepared timbers, there is an emphasis on its own uniqueness and origins that brings 'nature' into the room.

The Japanese house invites in nature by other means as well. Sometimes through the entrance, or hallway, which is considered transition space and is often connected to a veranda (*engawa*). Alternatively, a town-house (*machiya*) inner courtyard is seen as more of an outdoor room than a yard, with full height screens, as opposed to windows, allowing, when open, the inner garden courtyard to become part of the house. In his excellent book, *A Japanese Touch for Your Home* (1982), Koji Yagi explains that the garden acts like soft green 'walls' rather than being a separate open area. The distinction between the public and private areas in Western houses and gardens is clear, and we know whether we are inside or outside a house. However, the Japanese encourage a certain ambiguity. The Japanese garden is to be viewed from inside the house, looking out, as opposed to the Western tradition of the garden being primitive. Considering the detached nature of many English and American gardens, there seems a lot that can be learnt from this.

Many trees and plants in Japanese gardens are positioned with reference to internal sight-lines, reinforcing the connection between house and garden. The most private room, often occupied by an older family member, faces the garden, and care and effort is put into making the secluded garden elevation beautiful. Conversely, the street elevation is kept unostentatious and more low-key. Our Western ideas reverse this, with the 'back' elevation devoid of the grandiose details on view at the façade or street side.

The Japanese veranda developed not as an external 'sun' room but to provide weather protection for the *shoji* translucent sliding doors – originally lined with paper – that extend each room into the garden. It was an intermediate zone, where shoes can still be worn and business conducted with non-intimate visitors. The veranda also provides an external corridor, allowing the house to spread over a wide area with increased sound privacy. It almost separates the house into a series of pavilions. Usually these external veranda/corridors are raised about 45cm (18in) off the ground. If kept at ground-level, they are designed to be part of the garden and become more like a terrace, in which case they would be made from gravel. Handrails were rarely used, emphasizing the openness to the garden and importance of the view. The Western tradition of verandas sees them more as a transition space, an all round protection zone from the weather, with visitors fully fenced in.

It is not only the public face of the Japanese house that is kept unassuming, but the interior too is ordered and uncluttered. Their perception of beauty is influenced by Buddhist values of oneness with nature and quiet meditation, the emptying of the mind. Words such as *wabi* (quietness with simplicity) and *sabi* (elegance through economy) don't have Western counterparts but well describe the important Japanese sensibility when establishing personal priorities in house design.

The Japanese house is carefully designed on a grid pattern and made with timber posts and beams so the walls become merely infill. This means that the

In the Japanese house the veranda – here in bamboo and wood – has a surprising value. It provides an external corridor, increasing the circulation space of the house; it also acts as a transition zone, both public and private, and provides weather protection for the shoji *translucent sliding doors, allowing the garden to become part of the interior on demand.*

internal structure can be lightweight and flexible, allowing for a change in room size depending on requirements or activities. This is especially vital in a society where manners and polite awareness of others is fundamental, and in which privacy takes on quite a different meaning. The *tatami* floor-mat became the planning module (classed as enough room for one person to sleep), around which the structure or posts are positioned; because the interiors are sparsely furnished the 'screens' themselves create all the major visual elements. Without the need for heavy furniture, especially chairs, tables or beds, an unusual and intense relationship develops between the pillars, ceiling and 'mobile' walls.

Somewhat naturally the screens evolved as an exercise in geometric elegance with minimal use of materials as well as an emphasis on fine construction, complex joints and skilled craftsmanship. As they all join together in such a variety of constructions their design has to be carefully considered, not only from an aesthetic viewpoint but also with an eye to cost.

In earlier times the tatami *floor-mat became the major planning module around which the posts and walls are positioned, as seen in this Japanese teahouse in the Uransenke Chanoyu Center, Manhattan, New York. The walls are composed with geometric precision. A post (here a 'dressed' tree trunk) is introduced as a symbol of nature.*

81

RIGHT
The geometry of the grid is a particular interest of mine, beautifully demonstrated here in the window glazing by Japanese architect Hiroynki Ishida. I especially enjoy the order and calmness it creates; its sense of continuum and lazy inevitability. Paradoxically, only in its disruption do these very qualities become apparent.

ABOVE
As there was little furniture in older Japanese houses the space under the stairs was a chance to create a valuable storage area. The geometry of neat, rising steps linked well with that of the rectangular grids into which the wall screens were divided. This staircase design, in a kitchen in Gloucestershire, is a project of mine, inspired by its Japanese forebears.

The screens' secondary, or alternative function, is as sliding 'doors'. They provide closet space in which to place mobile furniture, bedding and so on. The few odd exceptions to all this illusion and disguise are the staircase and kitchen cupboards, which remain visible and are expressed as part of the wall. They perform as both architectural fittings and furniture at the same time.

The use of the grid in the geometry of these wall screens is a particular interest of mine. I enjoy the order and calmness the grid creates, its continuum as well as its sense of completeness or perfection, which introduces a lazy kind of inevitability. In some ways the grid pattern concurrently sets up a kind of tyranny with a parallel desire for disruption. It becomes a game in which enjoyment comes from where to break the rigid 'rules' that have been set up by introducing interruption. The grid is a designer's dream, especially if one enjoys working with asymmetry. I have applied the grid system many times, in particular to staircases, cupboards and large pieces of furniture, as well as for more general and widespread design, such as that of the ground-floor plan itself.

The culture of smallness is an aspect of Japanese influence that I find interesting. The esteem of the miniature in Japan has great lineage. Apart from a pause earlier this century, when admiration for the Western path of industrial modernization and its associations with largeness of scale was predominant, this admiration is as strong as ever and returning with renewed gusto. In the West smallness is often associated with 'poverty', but I suspect a new attitude is now afoot. As Kenji E. Kuan, Japanese director of G. K. Industrial Design Associates, says, 'Smallness in itself does not equate luxury. But when every possible wisdom and consideration are packed into a small space, creating an expensive and rich and abundant world, in a small thing, then smallness equates luxury.' Small houses, if well planned, can be compact, convenient and efficient. Largeness can be equated, he says, with, 'unrefinedness and be aggressive and wasteful'. In Japan, where traditional craftsmanship concerned itself with logical planning of structural elements to satisfy the enjoyment of miniaturization, people were able to live comfortably in confined spaces.

Most of us are mesmerized by elaborate craftsmanship and affected by the care and thought, concentration and dedication that are its preconditions. It links us emotionally to objects or space and lifts our spirits. We can feel the mind and body satisfyingly at work, together, and that is when perfection is possible. I often say that if the thinking part is not right, that is the design, then no matter how good the craftsmanship, the results are not satisfying. Optimal end results are achieved not with minimum effort but with maximum thinking, the necessary precondition for perfection. When there is a sense of economy and clarity of structure, craftsmanship has the chance to express real beauty with a sense of completeness. An elegant design is surely one where there is a sense of economy, of using thriftiness to maximize the essence of the design and achieve a compactness within its terms of reference.

One of the best historical roots of smallness is in the art of Bonsai. This is the method of artificial cultivation that produces miniature trees – or plants – that have the characteristics of larger ones, with gnarled trunks and elegant and developed structures. To quote Kenji E. Kuan again: 'Encapsulated in this tiny space is the space and time of nature. The Bonsai artist is a designer. While creating a miraculous harmony between tree and trunk, the branch and the pot, he must watch the strength of root and attend to the growing. By learning to avoid monotony he creates endless variations, i.e. nature which can be transported anywhere, even indoors – this is Bonsai.'

This capacity and love of miniaturization is also like a realm that children inhabit; as well as a home for the child in us. Witness the number of fairy tales set in small-scale worlds. It is a convenient way of controlling and managing reality, which reminds us of one of the main functions of the house: to act as an emotional, psychological and spiritual shelter. I go on to explore those aspects of the house later, for adults need this umbrella of security too.

The remarkable quality of early Japanese woodwork is world renowned for its daring shapes, bold geometric forms and the intellectual vigour behind its construction of joints. Wood is a warm, heartening material, unlike metal, which can be cold, with unpredictable qualities through its organically 'grown' nature.

3

THE CONTEMPORARY HARDWORKING HOUSE, ROOM BY ROOM

The California Media Kitchen, showing the curved cool cupboard, central island in the foreground and appliance stack on the far right. The choice of materials was designed to suit Californian light.

Kitchen

One of my key ideas has been how to plan a kitchen in order to build an harmonious relationship between specialized pieces of furniture, each chosen to perform a major kitchen function and link them to the scale of the room. This giant court cupboard was made for a twelfth-century stone abbey, combining old and new in a functional yet aesthetic piece.

I F this book has any underlying themes then they are about how to create homes that are humane, work well and reflect our individuality. This means not just solving the problem of how to make the house work as a whole but also showing that there is some element of pleasure, joy and satisfaction in both the doing and the end-results. My own experience is greatest with kitchens because this is where there is the most need for design assistance. It is the hardest-working room in the majority of homes. In *The Art of Kitchen Design* (1994) I wrote about the new role of kitchens as sociable rooms redefined after the middle years of the century when the focus had been more on the kitchen's labour functions. Certainly, wherever there is space, the new kitchen is both a sociable room and a work room. As this trend develops along the lines of a medieval Great Hall, a multi-purpose room, we surely need to give it a brand-new name to emphasize these non-culinary activities.

In this newly defined space guests are welcomed, fed and entertained. But it is a private space, too. Families gather in it, our children do their homework at the kitchen table, we adults read in it and deal with our paperwork – the installation of a kitchen desk is always a popular item if there is room. A mass of other activities take place in the kitchen, too, from shoe cleaning to jam making and children's parties. Essentially, every kitchen is unique not only for its size, location and architectural envelope but also in the requirements of its owners or users. In trying to move towards a new definition of the kitchen, in those illustrated here I have used titles that reflect its expanded activities and include the individuality of the location and home owners. But let's first take a brief look at its historical precedents.

HISTORY

The history of the kitchen is parallel to, indeed mirrors, that of our domestic and social life. It maps changing attitudes to hospitality, and widening knowledge of cooking, plus an increasing range and choice of diets and use of available foods. It has also emerged from our evolving sense of design, the current state of technology and the history of trade, especially the spice trade and its impact on our cultural, including culinary, traditions. In essence the history of the kitchen is a record of the changing patterns of human behaviour, both private and public, charted in what I consider to be the key social and functional room of the house.

I have described this all at some length in *The Art of Kitchen Design*, so I shall briefly summarize my views again here. In essence, my belief is that the kitchen is effectively a sociable space, its origins lie in the hearth; cooking and eating are largely group or family activities; when done alone they become

purely functional and provide a somewhat incomplete experience that is better for being shared.

It was the Dutch in the seventeenth century who first consciously developed the concept of domesticity in the Western sense. The formation of a separate kitchen came about due to the convergence of a series of social forces. The predominantly Calvinistic religious mentality prevalent in the Netherlands at the time advocated simplicity, thrift and the importance of family values. For Dutch merchants who spent months at sea, home was the refuge to which they could return, the place to refuel, emotionally as well as physically.

With the master of the house often absent for long periods of time, the mistress of the household took over its management, running it herself with a sense of decorum, order and femininity, so creating a new form of domesticity. The servants, or assistants, who were employed to help with the household chores, particularly in the kitchen, did not stop her involvement in domestic activities, but released her to run a more orderly household. The taming, or civilizing, of the kitchen came about from her participation.

In this eighteenth-century painting by Edward Bird, The Reception in the Kitchen Following the News of Bobby Shandy's Death, *despite the upsetting occasion the atmosphere remains equable. Masters and servants converse together in this friendly but spacious kitchen beside an open fire–cooking range, capacious dresser and well-worn flagstone floor.*

During the late seventeenth and early eighteenth centuries the civilized ideas of the Dutch bourgeoisie penetrated England. The Age of Reason, as the period is known, created a mental climate eager for progress. Increasing craft and technological skills and improved transportation and education changed notions of what was civilized. The concept of comfort started to develop, and the interior design of homes became a major activity in the light of these developments.

Although cooking itself remained primitive and the idea of the domestic open hearth with its attendant smoke and inefficiency was still prevalent until the 1850s, homes in general became closer to our modern notions of comfort. The development of the new yeoman class in the country and the newly rich mercantile bourgeoisie in the massively expanded cities, created in the confident but adaptable Georgian style, formalized for the first time a design language usable for every room in the house and capable of suiting all tastes. This incorporated both grand and vernacular versions of stylistic add-ons that ranged from Gothic to Chinoiserie; from oak country furniture to elegant mahogany carved bookcases for grand rooms. It enabled a lifestyle package to be exported successfully to Britain's colonies and neighbours.

The kitchen may have been a servants' room in the grand stately homes' restaurant–kitchen, but elsewhere it was still a sociable place with a sense of order. The rural derivative, the farmhouse kitchen, had more of a 'family', democratic or bucolic feel to it. As I explored earlier in the Country Life Revisited section of part one, this is the model kitchen to which many of us aspire today.

By the mid-nineteenth century the North American interest in housework and efficiency evolved due to a shortage of servants and the high price of labour. Thus the easy-to-maintain home, using design in conjunction with ergonomics – the method or science of measuring efficiency – became a popular goal. Catherine Beecher in *A Treatise on Domestic Economy* (1849) discussed the kitchen in some detail, suggesting a planned relationship between the sink and stove that also contained new ideas of storage. Other innovations followed, and by the twentieth century, along with the industrialization of so many of our everyday objects, the kitchen became a product that had to be marketed: a way of selling the vast quantities of furniture and household objects that the increasing number of factories found it economic to produce, rather than focusing on the best design for the space and clients' needs.

The science of marketing has taken over to a large extent when it comes to the design of our kitchens today. But real design does exist. Individual carpenters, furniture-makers and designers can offer this option, but they too, to some degree, have to follow the design parameters set by the market leaders, whose impact is similar to the pattern books of the eighteenth century. Being outside this process is hard, but I have tried it myself, and it is possible. Case histories follow of my own attempts to offer an alternative way of creating kitchens that are a genuine response to each client's individuality, the architectural needs of the space and my own response to them.

THE SOCIABLE KITCHEN

The clients' main form of relaxation is to cook for friends and family after a busy week in London or abroad, but they dismissed the idea of a dining room even though there was enough space for several. The key idea was to make a working kitchen within a 'sociable' space; to cook in the company of friends and family.

A separate, enclosed space overlooking the sociable areas was the final choice, comprising a three-quarter circular counter of English oak and elm, some of it painted, with a transparent screen overhead and a single point of access. All cooking activities are contained within the circular counter, with different levels of work-top height for particular tasks. There is an end-grain maple chopping block with a stainless-steel pull-out waste bin, accessible from three sides, for preparing food, a low-level vegetable prep sink and a

The kitchen within. A loose, circular counter provides an enclosure in which to work while looking out across the generously sized 'sociable' parts of the room, enabling culinary activity to be undisturbed by traffic and conversation to continue uninterrupted by the cooking process.

The robustness of the materials and furniture design had to work with that of the room, where exposed structure, large stone-mullioned windows and a beamed ceiling could easily over-power too delicate furniture. The kitchen was placed in the old chapel of a thirteenth-century abbey so space was plentiful enough for a generous walk-in central island. The rood screen above eye-level creates a muted sense of enclosure.

ABOVE
The detail of the rood screen is made from acid-etched glass, which hides the metal hanging rack and lighting gantry. The coat of arms is taken from an original design found at the abbey.

The Aga cooker, with a back-up electric cooktop, also provides the hearth replacement and with its steel canopy, fitted above for removing cooking fumes makes a suitably imposing presence in the large space.

larger double sink for washing-up. The dishwasher is loaded from the outside perimeter adjacent to the dining table. The Aga and cooking facilities are housed below a large steel canopy and sit, appropriately, against the wall, along with the American fridge, likewise in need of wall space. For storage there is a special cool larder built into a dividing wall, and near the dining table a giant court cupboard, which provides extra fridge space as well as the perching position that's always welcome in a sociable kitchen. The table, which can seat 14, makes even a room like this seem a little cramped. I agonized over this; there's only just over a metre (3ft) between one end of the table and the circular counter. But I was assured by my clients that this was not only satisfactory but added incident to the room as well. Too much distance between furniture can be discomforting and uncosy.

THE CALIFORNIAN MEDIA KITCHEN

Palo Alto, California, is a clean, elegant mini–city near Stanford University, in the heart of Silicon Valley. It seemed appropriate to acknowledge its topography with a deconstructed masonry structure. The clients work at the cutting edge of technological innovation, and so the kitchen reflects this with the very best of media equipment. One end of the room is devoted to a cabinet designed for a Home Theatre with space aplenty for sofas, chairs, rugs and a fireplace to enrich the experience further.

At the kitchen end of the room, the design works geometrically to facilitate ease of movement as well as to encourage as much activity as possible in the centre of the room. The spatial relationship of the sink, the fridge and the cooking area is conveniently close and responds to the chosen architectural *esprit de corps*. There is a window in front of the sink and a descending staircase into the basement behind the fridge. The central island with multiple functions includes a range as well as storage of various kinds, preparation space and built–in sociability. For storage and serving drinks, there is an alcove at

BELOW LEFT
The curved cool cupboard, made of cherry, provides intermediate-temperature food storage and conforms to the Soft Geometry layout, making the journey through the room pleasurable.

BELOW RIGHT
View showing curved-fronted sink cabinet. Its fulcrum is situated at the centre of the island chopping block. Easy movement around the island is consequently encouraged and the open area underneath the circular section reduces the feeling of being boxed in.

The room is divided into three activity zones to make a communicative, multipurpose space – the food preparation 'circle', as seen in the foreground, the fridge, prep sink and auxilliary work-top in the centre and the media room space with television and fireplace shown in detail on page 138.

the entrance to the main room, behind the cool cupboard, known jokingly as the Butler's Pantry.

As for aesthetic decisions, we had a lot of fun tossing around ideas. As Palo Alto is on the San Andreas faultline, Californian-earthquake style was one suggestion, with new elements added whenever there is volcanic activity. This reflects the core idea of allowing each piece of furniture to be individual in its own right. The centre island is a Victorian, Neo-classical work-horse, the sink

a curve-fronted stainless-steel structure, and the curved cool cupboard neon-lit to display food and dry goods like a neighbourhood store. A prep sink and concrete work-top supported by a tubular leg made from copper, much like a garage workbench, echoes the hardworking concrete tiles on the floor. The patinated-copper central extractor above the island brings several elements together in a stimulating mix of materials. The uniqueness of each piece makes the entire space more individual, something not so readily available from standard factory-made furniture.

The Butler's Pantry. Not for butlers, but for serving drinks, storing dishes and glasses, along with a hidden second dishwasher and icemaker. It is positioned conveniently near the dining area.

THE GREAT HALL KITCHEN

The room chosen by Howard and Jan Jones for their kitchen happened to be one end of the entrance hall of their nineteenth-century converted coach house and stables. We took out the low loft ceilings and one dividing wall, and – hey presto! – we had a commodious space with the opportunity for natural light from skylights and a real chance to do something vigorous in this attempt to get away from the erstwhile cramped and dark rooms. We realized, too, that because the roof thus became such a dynamic feature, it felt more like a Great Hall, or mini-house, than just a kitchen. Doubling as the entrance hall, this synchronized well with the idea of a room that was welcoming, a mecca of different activities, somewhere to hang out a little – and I should say here that the clients are musicians.

This kitchen is a place to cook and to pass through, both across and along its length, to reach a recording studio just beyond circular French doors. The key to the design was the management of people moving throughout the corridor-shaped space. Hence the circular form of the island, with its

BELOW
Detail showing how the cabinetry in the room works to back up the central island drum wtih a low-level work-top and a tall convex storage cupboard. In the left, foreground, is a three-sided circular cupboard, 31.5in (800mm) in diameter, that acts as the attractive transition piece defining the separate zones.

RIGHT
The kitchen here is divided into three zones: the soft area with dining table in the foreground, at the centre the food preparation and traditional kitchen activities, and at the back the entrance hall. You have to walk through the kitchen to reach the main house, emphasizing its welcoming aspects that set the tone for the house. In the loft area Paul Jobst's metalwork screen is visible.

The view into the garden terrace, showing the Japanese-inspired key window. The circular stone cart-wheel floor was positioned to create a hardwearing surface under the cooking and washing-up areas, where timber would not have stood up well to heavy use.

ABOVE

The table was positioned near the garden and in the area of greatest natural light below the two largest skylights. In summer, with the French doors open, this close connection to the garden makes it a popular place to sit.

immediate cluster of associated furniture, the low-level work area, sink cabinet and circular storage cupboard. Even when kitchen activities are in full swing, it has to be possible to walk its length without impediment; as the room is just under 3m (llft) wide this was quite a challenge.

From the start Howard, who, with Jan, owns a modest art collection, was keen to have creative input from artists as well as designers. Being highly sympathetic to Arts and Crafts ideals myself, I saw this as an ideal opportunity to involve a wider range of input. Lucy Turner, the Australian artist who painted the furniture, and Paul Jobst, who designed and made the high-level metal screen and lights, were the chief contributors, but furniture-makers Nigel Brown and his team equally deserve to be included in the elevated category of artist-craftsmen, in particular Patrick Warnes.

The three different zones of activity – the cooking and preparation facilities at the core, the relaxation and dining area at the garden aspect and the entrance hall at the far end – give a distinct order to the space. Once the ergonomics of the plan were established, then the rest became a combination of enjoyment, of harmonizing materials, textures and shapes, and using artistic licence in balance with the concept of comfort psychology. The kitchen hasn't yet had a song released in its name, but I believe one is planned!

THE KITCHEN IN TWO PARTS

This is an adaptation of an old idea. The separation of the wet kitchen and the cooking and dining area was a particularly common traditional practice in larger English farmhouses. The unmarried farmhands would have their clothes washed by the women of the house in a separate area, off the kitchen, known as a wet room. The kitchen therefore became the equivalent of a living room with a cooking range, backed up by a second scullery-cum-laundry. When I visited Alison and David Streatfeild-James they were already treating the two rooms in a similar way, but the main problem was insufficient space to house a sink cabinet, refrigerator and sofa in the 'living-room' kitchen. So rather than compromise by trying to squeeze in too much, we decided to opt for two separate kitchens.

Given that opening up the two rooms would gain little, we felt it worth respecting the existing architectural envelope of their Tudor manor house; knocking down walls to increase space can distort the character of an individual room, often disturbing its proportions and invalidating the use of some doorways and windows. It can also make the position and size of fireplaces awkward, and fill up all the corners – something I try to avoid. I was a little nervous about Alison walking next door every time she wanted to use the dishwasher, but she pointed out that she was already doing so and found this preferable to an overcramped kitchen. Certainly, positioning the table under the window turned meal-times into a real pleasure.

The main design innovation was the shape of the central island, generated by the circulation patterns; three circular work stations, their sizes dependent on how much space was available at different points in the kitchen, were joined together by a connecting triangular work-top. Each circle has one activity that relates to its size and work-top material. It allows Alison, and David, who cooks a lot at weekends, to prepare food together without getting in each other's way. As Alison became more enthusiastic about the design's living-room qualities, we upgraded her home desk into a more sophisticated home office with filing drawers and space for her computer.

The wet kitchen, known by its previous name, the pantry, has a more functional appearance and plenty of useful storage. A series of three shallow cupboards hug the wall with the deepest one at the centre. I couldn't resist having a little bit of fun on the food cupboard in the centre by using a carved cherry-wood panel inspired by Alison's Pharaoh-like hair! (I hope she will forgive me.) At a sensible height (1.05m/3ft 6in) a big, deep Belfast sink opposite allows for washing up the largest of pans without getting soaked. All too many sinks are shallow and narrow – and often set too low.

I went back a year or so after the kitchen was finished and asked Alison and David if they would do the same again, dividing the kitchen into two, and their reply was affirmative. It is particularly good to work with clients who can see no limits to what is possible, because the results are nearly always better. However, sometimes it's nice to be asked to do the impossible. Then I can justify my job as a designer a little more easily!

ABOVE
A desk was built into the design of this kitchen to enable household office tasks to be administered on the spot without the distraction of moving to a separate room. There is space to house the ubiquitous computer, as well as shelves for books and ornaments, drawers for filing household paperwork and a noticeboard.

LEFT
View of the sociable aspect of the main kitchen in the back, right-hand side of the picture, which provides maximum storage with minimum impact in a small room. By dividing the kitchen into two rooms we could include a sofa and dining table in this room.

ABOVE
A screen to replace the original corridor wall increased space and gave privacy and intimacy to the eating area.

BELOW
With no room for a central island, a peninsula with access from three sides provides an excellent alternative.

THE HARDWORKING KITCHEN

I certainly had to use all my design skills on this space and justify my claims to be a designer. The client was expecting her fifth child, and we had to plan a kitchen with a table for seven in a room measuring 3.6m (12ft) wide and 4.5m (15ft 9in) deep. The ergonomics had to be carefully worked out, so that there was maximum flow of activities between surfaces and minimum walking distance, allowing a positive advantage to be made of the somewhat constricting narrowness of the space.

As is often the case when making big demands on small rooms, architectural reorganization came to the rescue. By taking out the corridor wall, the space available was increased. Although this allowed us to dedicate it as surface to house a large grid cupboard for storage, the remaining area still had to be used as a corridor to access both a dining room and living room. I designed a curved hybrid settle, which doubled as a screen, to encapsulate the desire for privacy around the table and help to isolate the kitchen a little from the corridor. This also deflects the kitchen atmosphere from the hallway, so reinforcing its primacy as a thoroughfare.

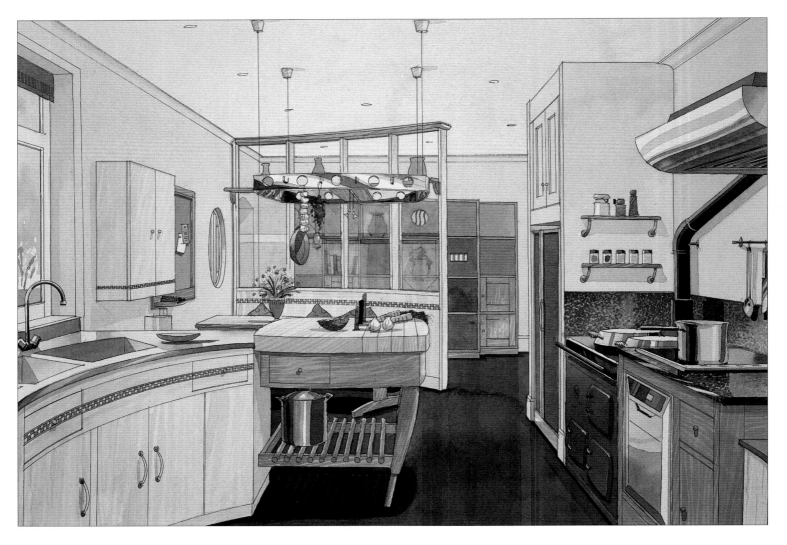

Ambiguity is a quality in furniture I enjoy and something of which I often make use. Is it more a screen, a settle or a room divider, a piece of furniture or an architectural fitting? By using acid-etched glass, which is translucent rather than transparent, by stopping the glass well below the ceiling line, by introducing a shelf at the top to add elements of display (like a dresser) and a curved shelf-top lower down on the corridor side to suggest the function of a console table, the pieces possess a polyglot quality.

Multi-functional furniture is a hallmark of a hardworking kitchen. Its only drawback is not to devalue usability by trying to make every piece so flexible that it carries out none of its appointed tasks efficiently and is overcompromised, like many so-called functional, fitted factory-made kitchens. There may be plenty of work-tops, but not much care has been taken over how the space will be used or enjoyed, sometimes creating a vacuous flexibility, in which the work-top space ends up as shelf space.

Making a hardworking kitchen is more than just designing for function; it's for enjoyment, too. That means introducing aesthetic qualities – natural materials, time-intensive craftsmanship, elegant details and, just as importantly, a sense of fun, movement and colour.

This bird's-eye view shows a plan designed to provide maximum countertop space that retains the sensibilities of a furnished room. A priority was a table to seat seven, which meant that quite a large percentage of floor space had to be set aside for this purpose.

UTILITY ROOM

In centuries past the grander houses divided a lot of the service activities we now cram into the kitchen among many separate rooms. Some were staff-orientated rooms, like the Butler's Pantry and the housekeeper's room, or connected to producing 'raw' food. Peter Brears, in his fascinating and scholarly account, the *Country House Kitchen, 1650-1900* (1996), describes the ideal kitchen in 1864 as comprising a few separate rooms: a scullery for washing dishes and cooking equipment, and preparing vegetables, game and fish; a pantry or dry larder for storing bread, pastry and cooked meats, butter and milk; a meat or wet larder; a game larder; a fish larder; a salting room; a bacon larder, usually a cupboard placed up high to attract warm air; a smoking house; a dairy; a bakehouse; an alehouse; a whole variety of cellars for storing wines and beers; a still-room for making pastry, cakes and biscuits; a series of demi-rooms for storage, such as a china, silver or linen closet, dry goods, preserves, household equipment and boot rooms, and finally a variety of servants rooms, divided into the 'men's side' and 'women's side'. Thus the kitchen was left free for roasting, cooking and preparation.

Today's needs are well catered for by a visit to the supermarket, where much of the preparation work has been done in factories, ready for us to consume without much ado. So the real purpose of a utility room is for storage. If it is to be used as a larder, though, the temperature must be quite cool, and the room itself should ideally face north in a northern climate and vice versa in a

The walk-through pantry. In this recent design a pantry was created by enlarging a corridor exit to the garden. The shelves are for storage of dry goods (a cool cupboard, out of the picture, for meats, cheeses and vegetables) and a banquette for sitting on while changing for the garden or pool. The shelves are simply constructed and the metal straps allow a lot of weight to be carried.

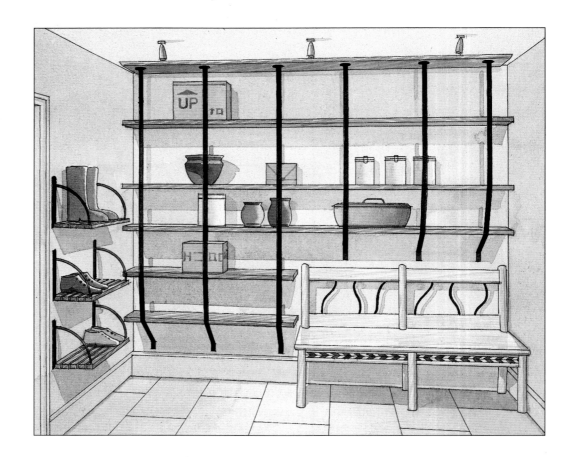

southern one. Slabs of marble or slate assist with maintaining the suitably low temperatures. And plenty of shelves, hooks, flyproof cages and baskets are vital, along with large storage tins to keep away mice. With our squirrel instinct, having a well-stocked larder brings a definite feeling of security, perhaps a residue from times past, when getting through the winter was hard. Like having a good pile of firewood, or savings in the bank, a full larder and a good supply of household goods is thoroughly reassuring. The room should now be seen in a new light and perhaps renamed the Household Supply Room.

LAUNDRY ROOM

A separate room for washing and ironing in a busy household is not so much a luxury as a necessity. Laundry and food preparation don't mix well. For a start most washing machines and driers are noisy; they also need their own sink and draining board. A commodious linen cupboard nearby is useful with, ideally, three, but at least two, laundry baskets for dirty linen – one for coloured items, one for whites and one for specials. A space for ironing is helpful too.

A room dedicated to laundry fits into the idea of the house working like a well-oiled machine; there is pleasure to be gained in being part of an efficient household. Where there is the natural momentum implicit in the easy, frictionless effort of precision engineering, the tedium of household chores is lessened a little. Besides good planning, the building of quality cabinets with the added luxury of true craftsmanship in robust and solid natural materials gives a feeling of efficiency combined with visual satisfaction. Why should the laundry be a crummy and dark space, a Cinderella room? We take a lot of pleasure from wearing clothes, and their maintenance should not be seen always in negative terms.

I have planned a number of laundry rooms. A deep generous sink – either stainless steel or fireclay (Belfast or London pattern) – is essential. Draining boards for scrubbing are necessary, too, ideally a minimum of 600mm (2ft) long on both sides. A raised-height washing machine, if it is a front-loading European type, is important because otherwise the stooping becomes tiresome. American top-loading machines are usually larger but have to go side by side with other equipment and are more suitable for families. Placing the drying machine underneath is a sensible option, otherwise raise it by around 600mm (2ft) and use the space beneath for drawers because it is used slightly less than other household utility appliances, especially in summer. One other vital requirement is a good clothes-hanging rack, attached to either the ceiling or the wall. The ceiling option is usually the more capacious, especially if the room is high. There are also a variety of extendable wall-mounted versions, but these are often quite small and inadequate given the new ecological awareness of using the dryer less and saving on electricity. Besides, hanging out clothes often avoids having to iron them.

The laundry room is less a luxury than necessity: capacious baskets for dirty washing, machine and tumbledryer stacked conveniently one above the other, saving valuable space for airing/storage. The cupboard fronts are staggered so as to preserve the small scale of the room. The one illustrated here doubles as a playroom too.

Dining Room

HISTORICALLY the dining room developed during the fifteenth century, when the Great Hall was stripped of its communal use. The grand family of the house had begun to move upstairs into the Great Chamber, a semi-private reception room – often furnished with an imposing four-poster bed – to which only an invited élite were allowed admittance. Visitors here were entertained at small tables, but it was clearly impractical for banquets. As the Great Hall turned increasingly into a space for servants and family retainers, this was no longer suitable for dining either. It became necessary to create a second chamber near to the Great Chamber, used exclusively for dining. But this was eventually seen as impractical when located too far from the kitchen and other public rooms, particularly after the 'enfilade' system became extinct, and privacy became a concept associated with the bedroom. Thus a separate dining room was created downstairs.

That the dining room grew from a communal Great Hall and a bedchamber that was semi-private is interesting because to this day it remains a 'domesticated' room, albeit falling more in line with its 'public' persona. It often remains a comfortable space with plenty of soft furnishings and prestigious furniture. Paintings and *objets d'art* enhance it as a reminder of its past pedigree as a place for banquets, grand occasions and showing off family assets, as providing a sense of history, or connection, to the wider cultural world.

ABOVE

The Great Hall at Dorney Court, a sixteenth-century Tudor manor house in Buckinghamshire. By the time it was built the Great Hall was already going out of fashion as a communal living/cooking/dining area, becoming more of a room for household servants and public occasions, rather than for family or private eating.

RIGHT

The contemporary version: a dining room incorporated into the kitchen, mixing exposed beams and stripped floorboards with more contemporary furniture, the kitchen neatly zoned off but still integral to the room, making a friendly, practical and sociable space. Cooking for many is now not just a chore but at weekends, in particular, a hobby.

Formal with a certain gran-
diloquence that is ideal for
stylish entertaining, yet possibly
also more private and relaxed for
less lavish occasions. In this design
I have tried to balance the two.
Like the previous example, it is
part of a kitchen and has the
additional function as an entrance
hall (just out of the picture).

To have or not to have? I have engaged in this discussion with so many clients. Do we need dining rooms any more? Are they an unnecessary luxury? In smaller houses where there is a shortage of space and, in particular, when there is a small adjacent kitchen that is dysfunctional and could use the extra space, then the answer must be no. A generous-size, sociable kitchen is a priority – and the dining room is fair game for absorption; however, when a decent-size kitchen is a *fait accompli*, then a dining room is a bonus. Many larger houses have dining rooms that could hardly be used in other ways, so here there is no argument.

Although using the dining room is often hard on the feet, with masses of walking and getting up to fetch things we've forgotten just when we've started to eat, the pleasures of its inherited grandeur can make family occasions special. It allows for larger and more organized parties. Help can be hired for special occasions, so that we can live up to the occasion and enjoy our own dinner parties. Punctuating our lives with 'occasions' adds significance, and generous hospitality is a pleasure to give and receive.

A large dining-room table allows for laying out the best family china and making inventive, eye-catching displays in the centre. I always enjoyed setting the table as a child and expecting guests made this all the more exciting. The preparation of the food, the design of the table top, the most exciting details

ABOVE
This stunning chandelier was commissioned from Deborah Thomas. Made of chopped-up glass and secretly positioned, miniature low-voltage lights, it provides a central focus for the room.

RIGHT
Dining rooms are primarily places of entertainment, and as somewhere for special occasions the rich design here seems appropriate. At maximum capacity this table seats 24. Keeping guests entertained is helped by rich use of colour, shape and lighting. But it is also a practical space with wall and floor cupboards for storage and a contemporary sideboard.

OPPOSITE
The sideboard design, although devised to be visually striking, is equally based on functional requirements. A hot zone isolated within the granite surface keeps food warm. The tall drum is used to stack dining plates conveniently to hand while its top functions as a display surface for flowers or food. Chinacraft designed and supplied the table settings.

– use of colour, food presentation, best glasses and polishing the silver – made for a real balance of creativity and showmanship. This is part of the long human tradition of hospitality with its important mixture of sociability and prestige.

The design of the dining room shown here was a response to these issues; the family regularly entertains on a large scale. As they are connected to a successful china retail business they enjoy the experience of selecting the best china on the market and trying it out. With the table set, the room looks truly magnificent and makes guests feel thoroughly welcome. The furniture and design had to match up to this, and so the room is a little more theatrical in its design than the other rooms in the house. A highlight was a specially designed chandelier. Trying to keep 24 people happy, well-served and entertained means that this dining room has to have a slightly exaggerated sense of décor.

The dining room in general is one of the few genuinely public rooms left in the house; most other rooms now have private or multiple use. As it is a space for entertaining, then perhaps it is appropriate to build a sense of theatre into its design – in the choice of fabrics, colours and lighting. I think I have convinced myself that a dining room is a luxury I'd like, even if I enjoyed it mostly as a peaceful sanctum from the other more hectic and over-used sociable rooms of the house. I suspect the dining room often ends up as a reserve home office, or a room to lift the spirits for that quiet meal for two when all the children have gone out. But when all the family is at home, then they can enjoy its formal atmosphere too.

Drawing Room, Living Room and other Sociable Rooms

The illustration below is a design proposal for this hybrid room, part living room, part media room but with enough formality to be suitable for a certain amount of entertaining as well. The circular corner cupboard with sliding doors reveals a television; on the right is a capacious drinks cabinet, with side shelving for glasses and bottles — as well as a pull-out 'tray' at the front, which can be used for serving.

WHEN I first considered the rooms I would cover in the book I left out these sociable rooms on the basis that they aren't hard-working enough when set against the kitchen, bathroom and workshop or any component parts of the house, such as staircases, walk-in cupboards and fireplaces. But then I realized that it is a mistake to think that just because one of its functions is relaxation this doesn't negate the need for either careful thought about a room's design performance or an awareness that it has a more hardworking role to perform.

A living room needs to be a comfortable place where we can shelter in an upholstered cocoon with a sense of individual space. Historically it has moved away from its upper-middle-class predecessor, the grander and more public drawing room, towards being a more private space. Apart from when entertaining, it should be a tranquil room whenever possible. The television may

invade this sense of peace but not necessarily disrupt our personal privacy. Television can be, in one sense, like an open hearth or stove fire – a substitute for company, yet mesmerizing. In northern climates, long winter nights around the fire form an essential focus for evening life that we cannot achieve with central heating. From the design viewpoint, by taking away a fireplace altogether we are left with the classic furnishing problem that prevailed in the sixties – no obvious focus around which to centre our activities.

Where can we make our seating circle? It depends on the size proposed and orientation of the room. Some good historical examples can be seen in eighteenth- and ninteenth-century drawing rooms. By the nature of its size the drawing room had at least two or often three or more seating circles. The primary one was by the fireplace; a second would be near a window – usually enhanced by a window seat with a fine view; others were around circular tables, perhaps a small one for card-playing or a larger one on which to read

Reconciling the prevailing modern desire for expansive and liberating architectural spaces with the security and comfort associated with the more small scale is difficult. Here the vast double-height living room with gallery mezzanine, built under the direction of the LA office of Moore, Ruble, Yudell, allows for generously sized chairs, with intimacy preserved by careful lighting and the substantial nature of the fireplace. It remains essentially at its best in the daytime.

The salon at Aynho, 1835, by Lili Cartwright. The uses of a drawing room merged in the nineteenth century. In this case it was clearly used for musical evenings, games, such as charades (on the raised podium), cards and so on. The luxurious, large-scale carpet gave the room a comfortable, feminine atmosphere – closer to a drawing room than a library.

or write. Some seating circles such as at Aynho had a musical centre at one end or a games playing area, in this case a raised platform. The use of a drawing room in the nineteenth century seems to have almost merged with that of the library. But the drawing room remained more formal and graceful in its atmosphere, considered better suited to the purposes of entertaining than the library, which was increasingly for family use.

Leaving behind the finer distinctions of their correct names, the essence of both these glorious rooms is flexibility. Seating circles were moved and formed according to the specific activity or need of the moment. The main fireplace circle was unlikely to be altered, so the heavier upholstered pieces of furniture were placed there. For the other seating groups, where the chairs were usually wooden framed and only semi-upholstered, arrangements were more temporary and responded to social needs. Board games, card games and reading, drinks, charades and larger social gatherings could all be accommodated with relative ease.

The decoration of the drawing room relied more on fabrics than other rooms in the house: luxurious carpets, generous curtains for the large and probably numerous windows, copious upholstered sofas and armchairs. The extravagant use of design, colour and texture provided the opportunity to achieve decorative effects and create the type of style and comfort wanted by the lady of the house. Feminine instincts also held sway in the smaller living room and so had a warmth and cosiness that made it more comfortable than the other rooms in the house.

For most of us today these distinctions may be of only passing interest for we don't have the space or time to spare for such a grand life, but it is fascinating to know from where some of our ideas and ways of living have come. Contrary to certain assumptions, gracious drawing rooms, for all their perceived space, were working rooms. They were planned sparsely, with elegant furniture, to allow flexibility of use. One large room in the house that can be used flexibly is a valuable asset; indeed a necessity if we wish to give parties or entertain.

Finally, a word about upholstery. The fabric of either a drawing or living room will get a lot of use. Fortunately, the worn-out look is fashionable today and part of the need for what I describe as 'assumed heritage'. Witness the success of 'shabby chic', or of the US Sofa Company, whose whole marketing plan is based on a worn look – not to mention the general love of aged paint effects and stone-washed fabrics. Companies such as British designers Mulberry have been developing superb collections of fabrics, clothes and accessories that reach the comfort zone effortlessly. Subtle, unchallenging but with a distinct almost subliminal familiarity their fabrics and designs recall past times. They have inherited Laura Ashley's mantle – a romantic style using natural fabrics, initially based on nineteenth-century designs – but work at a more understated level, retaining a sense of Englishness from years ago but injecting enough of the new to avoid being classed as reproduction.

ABOVE
Planning inevitably responds to the features of any room. In my own living room the window seat is a favoured spot; the other is by the fireplace, thus splitting the seating circle in two. Lightweight movable chairs help us transfer orientation easily.

LEFT
In this room in Christopher Nevile's own house the fireplace and overmantle offer a strong presence. On close inspection the carvings reveal an original contemporary interpretation of the traditional fireplace surround.

111

Library–Study

THE domestic library was ostensibly an eighteenth-century invention, created as it was in the Age of Reason, when learning, with its emphasis on the development of a scientific mentality, was considered both fashionable and progressive, so any well-to-do family needed the social and intellectual accoutrement of a well-stocked library. It was a status symbol, a sign of sophistication and of access to the world of ideas, culture and civilized values. Gradually a library became more affordable as literacy expanded; books became cheaper, and titles were published on a much wider range of subjects. Most eighteenth-century libraries had at least two or three writing desks and comfortable chairs arranged in seating circles. The implication was that the library involved sociable activity, a place not just for private study. There was a genuine and popular dedication to the study of books.

In the nineteenth century the library lost its role as a focus for scholastic studies. Losing its atmosphere of learning, it became more of a family room,

BELOW

Books do furnish a room, but how and where to store them? Here's one way of creating copious storage for books in a tall room. The ladder moves on a rail placed in front of the mid-height counter, so that no book is ever out of reach.

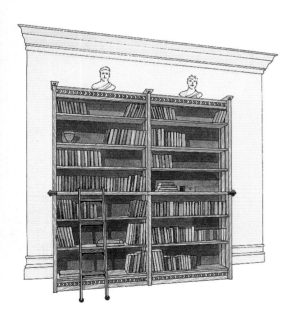

RIGHT

This design attempts to create a modern library–study. Warm colours with a well-balanced sense of comfort are balanced by the giant, cool and restrained charcoal drawings by the artist. Easy chairs, around a fireplace, with a fireseat provide a second focal point.

LEFT
At the client's special request,
an elm and sycamore lectern, or
reading-desk, with three drawers,
was made for the library–study so
that reading, or referencing, could
be carried out standing up, providing
an option to full-time, seated desk
work. An old-fashioned item of
furniture, it is nevertheless practical
and eye-catching.

ABOVE
My design for the desk and bookcases, in elm and sycamore, adds
a sobre quality to the rich colour
of the walls and vibrant oriental
carpet that graces the floor,
balancing traditional and modern
references. The curved desk hugs
the bookcase end of the room,
leaving circulation area by the
window or space for an easy chair.
The pendant overhead lights add
a touch of modern grandeur.

albeit still surrounded by the veneer of books. As the drawing room began to be kept for strictly formal occasions and was dominated by a more feminine sensibility, the library evolved a somewhat masculine ambience but with a distinct family orientation. It was less decorated, or composed, not so inhibited as the drawing room with its grand furniture and furnishings.

The term library today is used in the sense of a library–study. The presence of books in any room, particularly in voluminous quantities, suggests culture and learning and produces a correspondingly highbrow, scholarly atmosphere, as if all those condensed thoughts encapsulated in the pages are ready and waiting and permeate the room even before a book is opened. It is not surprising that many of us aspire to having a library, where the serious business of reading books can raise our spirits by taking our thoughts into the realm of the imaginary and away from the sometimes dogged realities of the present.

The two library–studies illustrated have an added function, inevitably because they are 'home offices'. They have a serious work function and as such spoil the slightly ethereal quality attributed to their historical predecessors. Nevertheless there are a few ways in which a sense of ease and civility can be ensured. By retaining a working fireplace and its associated paraphernalia – a fireseat, a mantlepiece with a centralized picture positioned above it and handmade fire equipment – and by adding generous, comfortable and perhaps slightly shabby armchairs, a worn-looking Persian carpet, freestanding desk and bookshelves, all of which encourages a more relaxed atmosphere. A few silver trophies or marble busts and photographs of school teams provide instant credibility and a final expression of tradition and respectability.

Few of us need libraries these days because the primacy of books as vehicles for information storage is gone; computers with floppy disks have taken over that role. Nonetheless a private study is a real bonus for any household. My brother Rupert, short of space in his small seventeenth-century Sussex cottage and wanting to retain its integrity, built a new, separate library barn, in the manner of seventeenth-century oak-framed construction. Instead of having his study separate he divided off a section within the space for a study, with a raised loft for his three children as a combined study/computer area, leaving the main area for sociable activities, which may include performing plays and musical evenings, exactly the kind of activities for which the Victorian library would have been used. Thus the idea of a large multipurpose family space with a more evocative atmosphere than a typical nursery or living room is seen to be thoroughly modern and civilized. It is in appearance a little like a medieval Great Hall but in its use it is a Victorian library, which is quite an achievement.

This all-purpose room, built by my brother Rupert and his wife, Jan, is known as the Library Barn. It incorporates a loft area for his children to use for homework and computer work, two bays for study downstairs and a generous fireside seating circle as well as a dining area.

Hallway

HE hallway is a space that has been forgotten or ignored by many of us in recent years. It has been squeezed out to give space to other rooms and is thoroughly undervalued and historically misunderstood. It has enjoyed a long and venerable history, adapting to various different uses over time. The hall-house, in medieval times effectively a one-room house, sometimes with a sleeping chamber and a room for storage or animals on either side, was the most common dwelling. The nobility, with their grander properties, centred activity around the Great Hall, and, by the fourteenth century, wealthier families had moved their private life into upstairs chambers. This left the rump of the household using the hall as a communal all-purpose space, which must have made for a lively and hectic atmosphere, particularly in winter with the advantage of warmth as the giant fireplace there was the major source of heat for the household.

As specialist rooms began to develop so the hall's multifarious uses diminished until eventually, by the eighteenth century, it was largely a room for welcoming visitors. It retained, though, the vestiges of its earlier communal use by being a focal-point for householders and guests. This is clear from the continued inclusion of a fireplace in a central position, and wherever possible the hall was still large enough to accommodate several awaiting visitors. It was considered socially necessary to have a room where guests could wait temporarily, to provide privacy for the household and act as a threshold to protect the use of other rooms.

One of the main repercussions of building an upstairs chamber was the need to house the staircase. This led to the development of a double-height space with a gallery above it. A gracious staircase that ascended with ease made the hall not just a thoroughfare but often the place for the most expensive joinery in the house. This was often revved up for visitors' benefit by wooden panelling and complex carvings. *Vis-à-vis* decoration, the hall also took on the role of integration. As it connected all the major rooms of the house, it had to reflect and assimilate, set the tone for the different sizes, characters and uses of its other parts. It was no longer a room as such, but its use for circulation meant it could be a place to linger before entering a 'social' room; and its fireplace was therefore a necessary focal-point. The hall was the great welcoming zone, and, conversely, the place where the family gathered for heart-rending departures, bad news or reunions – even just to shelter from a summer shower. The hall was seen by early Arts and Crafts architects, particularly Voysey and Prior, as an important room, where a good family or collective atmosphere could be fostered in the house. They always allowed in their plans for a generous hall.

In the USA the use of the hall in the early New England salt-boxes was as a sociable space. This combined with a dislike of corridors (because they wasted space) led to the development of open plan. The medieval hall-house is its antecedent. Generally open-plan houses are now being modified to deal with problems of noise or sound privacy and the disorientation that large non-specific, all-purpose spaces can cause. Rooms need a focus, whether it be a window, a view or a fireplace, a piece of furniture or a style of decoration. Hallways do not have these requirements and, I suspect, will begin to be re-continued with generous proportions as a civilized part of a well-designed house.

Another source of the renewed popularity of the hallway is the rise of interest in *feng shui*, the Chinese art of the science of place. It satisfies our yearning to find a deeper level or explanation for interior design, beyond questions of style or function. And it carries us into a mysterious territory, where our inside environment can release special energy, understand hidden forces and negative elements and better connect us as individuals to our homes. Rather than attempting to explain it here, Derek Walters' The *Feng Shui Handbook* (1991) provides an extremely good summary and demonstrates how it works. *Feng shui* is a fascinating

My own version of a Japanese-inspired way of using a staircase for storage. The geometry has a pleasing sense of completeness. Under the stairs drawers fit neatly beneath the steps, whereas these compartmentalized storage units provide a stylish, simple and functional solution, the design of which echoes the lines of the bannisters and stair treads. The stairs are also used for perching on to integrate the hallway into part of what is essentially a small kitchen.

BELOW
The hallway is a good starting place to apply the principles of feng shui. Mirrors can deflect chi, the vital, natural energy currents that need to be considered to establish favourable locations, as they intensify or redirect the image of anything that they reflect. They can provide a welcome for visitors as well as a defence against unwelcome ones.

OPPOSITE
This screen divides the kitchen, forming a hall-seat to remove shoes, perch or make phone calls. Its curves suggest and assist movement. On the reverse, the geometry makes a console table for flowers.

topic of study that will alter our view of the built environment in the West. The hall is considered an important space because it is seen as a facilitator, directing outside energy, or chi, through the house. *Feng* and *shui* translate roughly as wind and water respectively. Both imply flow or movement.

There are three main schools of thought that form its structure – and all emanate from precepts laid down in the ancient and sacred Chinese religious text *Li Shu* or the *Book of Rites*, itself concerned with the harmony of heaven, earth and nature. The Form School of *feng shui* is concerned with large-scale scenic formation. The Compass School, or Furkien method, is based on using the points of the compass to survey the topography of the immediate landscape. The third 'school' is not so much a school of thought as a collection of adages, folklore and common sense that has been built up over time. *Feng shui* is an extraordinary collection of history and science, design ideas and practicality, contradictions and superstition all rolled into one philosophy. Derek Walters describes it as a guide to Chinese geomancy and environmental harmony.

The concept of *chi* has multifarious meanings in Chinese culture, but in *feng shui* it ostensibly means favourable currents, not just fresh air but also other positive energies, such as light, heat, human energy or the view of the outside. The hallway is the gateway to the house. It needs to provide both a welcome for, or positive impact on, visitors as well as acting as a potential defence from unwelcome forces. *Feng shui* practice prohibits the placing of staircases directly opposite either the front door, back door or windows. Interestingly, our practice in the West is in agreement, probably because ignoring this undervalues the hall's role as a space in its own right as well as its ground-floor functions as an important conductor into the main public rooms, which, more often than not, are on the ground-floor. A room with windows at opposite ends, a 'through' room has no fixed point, no sense of repose, and it creates unease.

Although I am not an expert on *feng shui*, I feel we have much to learn from its folklore, and its more subtle approach and practice. There are, for example, techniques for reorientating a home to fit the personalities of the people who live in it, a sort of *feng shui* horoscope. To a large extent we do this naturally in the West, without any formal system, but we lack the accumulated wisdom provided by ancient sages, rather as we undervalue or ignore old people or grandparents in the race for the new. We have great respect for old buildings but no living belief system within which to use this, and our architects and designers jettisoned a lot of it to create Modernism. With hindsight, from some perspectives this seems arrogant and wasteful of our past – not that the Chinese have done that much better, judging by the terrible destruction of the Cultural Revolution and its violent ideological implant through Marxism.

We all need to re-evaluate our history in order to establish continuity, and we in the West need to understand the more subtle forces that exist inside and outside our buildings. There may be a lot of voodoo and silliness on the fringes, but that doesn't mean that there is no truth in it or use for it. *Feng shui* doesn't just apply to hallways – its scope is the whole built environment – but the hall is certainly a sensible place to start.

Bedroom

The State Bedchamber at Osterley Park, London, showing the eight-poster bed designed (1775–6) by Sir Robert Adam. More commonly seen early four-poster beds began as a practical response to drafts, but quickly became glorified as symbols of power and wealth. These beds were not necessarily used for sleeping in, but more often the place from where the king, or notable, would receive visitors.

Now the ultimate inner sanctum of the house, the origins of the bedroom were as a sociable room, at least during the hours of daylight. The upstairs Great Chamber arrived around 1350 – but only for use by the masters of the house and, surprisingly, not just as a place for sleeping. It was very much a sociable room, a kind of combined upstairs living and dining room. It usually contained a grand bed, either for guests or the nobles of the household, and was the best or certainly most comfortable room in a fourteenth-century house. The bed itself, a four-poster with hangings both for privacy and to keep out draughts, had symbolic value. In an era when most people slept on straw-filled bundles, it signified wealth through its elaborate carvings, sumptuous materials and craftsmanship.

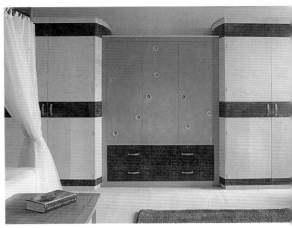

Contemporaneous sources make much of the relationship between dining and eating in bedrooms or great chambers. It required a retinue of servants to service. According to Dan Cruickshank in *The Name of the Room* (1993), night-time necessities might include a silver jug of beer, two large pots of wine and two kinds of bread all covered in napkins to protect them from the birds that flew freely around the lofty chamber. Breakfast apparently required 13 servants, including carvers, servers and cup bearers, and it was served on a trestle-table set up at the end of the bed with a breakfast board on top. Everything was pre-tasted, and a ritual of blessing and kissing was conducted by servants. A noble visitor would have his meal presented on a separate breakfast board.

Evening meals could also be served in the Great Chamber. The trend towards privacy continued, and the grander houses turned eating into a more formal activity. This saw the removal of the bed from the Great Chamber, which became to all intents and purposes an upstairs dining-cum-drawing room, and marked the development of the more precise bedchamber that was still a sociable room. The bed then clearly developed an aura of grandeur and

ABOVE LEFT
In a large room four-poster beds still provide a pleasurable feeling of enclosure as well as a sense of historical grandeur. I designed this bed in American walnut for a London house with a generous-size bedroom.

TOP RIGHT
The lightness of the posts and structure make the enclosure more suggestive than real.

BOTTOM RIGHT
The design for the wardrobes was divided into three sections to avoid making too massive an impact on the room. The middle section has circular icons of painted roses by Australian artist Lucy Turner.

OPPOSITE, TOP
The desire for simplicity in the bedroom, now the most private room in the house, sits comfortably with the Arts- and Crafts-inspired design with its inherent belief in simplicity, purity and country images. All the furniture was to be made without glue using natural wood finishes.

BELOW
In 1990 I designed a collection of bedroom furniture for Smallbone. The furniture was made in sycamore as a response to a desire for light woods in the bedroom, in a controlled balance between masculine and feminine influences. The four-poster adds a touch of romance, countered by the chequered bedcurtains. The dark-green, rather sombre walls are complemented by the paler, more frivolous ceiling colour.

importance. In France in the early seventeenth century, the king even attended parliament in his bed, which was placed on a dais underneath a curtained canopy!

As the impact of the ideas of the Italian Renaissance was felt in France and then reached England, an interesting dilemma developed: how to resolve the simultaneous desire for both display and privacy. Prestige and power, the inevitable concomitants of successful nobility, had to be balanced with a growing interest in comfort and seclusion, which in a watered-down way foreshadows a contemporary phenomenon. When rooms are open to public use, we design and perceive them in a different way. The kitchen, which now has a dual function, has grown to accept this and so has become larger, more prestigious and ambitious in its use of furniture and with a bigger share of the household decoration budget. Conversely, the bedroom has become increasingly private and so attracts less attention and investment.

By the 1650s one solution to achieving this balance of privacy versus display was the 'enfilade' plan, derived from the royal palace of Louis XIV at Versailles via the Palazzo Medici in Florence two hundred years earlier. This involved a vista of rooms with doors in parallel positions, progressing through each adjoining room towards the state bedroom, conferring increasing status on the occupants the nearer they were permitted access. From the salon, through the

ante-chambers, to the dressing rooms and minor bedchambers, the rooms became increasingly well furnished and culminated in the richly adorned main bedchamber with its adjoining alcove or closet and state bed.

The problem with the enfilade system was that the occupants were, in effect, sleeping in a corridor. Ironically, it wasn't until a purpose-designed corridor was either added later, as it was, for example, at Wilton House in Wiltshire, or adopted as a key element in the design of the house, that this problem was resolved. Along with allowing individual entry, servicing the rooms was thus more feasible, and this sounded the final victory for privacy; the bedroom of today remains an intimate place.

The bed, too, remains an important piece of furniture, and the enduring popularity of the four-poster is a reminder of the importance of historical precedent. Although beds are now more a symbol of sleep, relaxation – especially on slow, indulgent Sunday mornings – and sexual or marital togetherness, there remains a distinct sense of magic, status and privacy about four-poster beds. I have designed a number of them, as well as some half-tester beds, where the canopy extends halfway across the bed with posts only at the back. The half-tester has a similarly imposing presence but is open to the room and less dominant.

Qualities such as calmness and peacefulness are desirable in the bedroom and are strongly associated in our minds with the overriding modern desire for privacy. A recent design I carried out shows this: a few simply designed pieces of furniture with bare floor-boards and a rug are used to create a light and tranquil bedroom. The adjacent dressing room, separated with

BELOW
The ultimate luxury in any bedroom is a working fire. Here the fireplace surround and mantelpiece is made from mazur, birch and solid maple, which contrasts well with the colour and roughness of the exposed red-brick fireback, the warmth of the terracotta hearth and the coral-blackness of the cast-iron grate.

123

A walk-in closet in sycamore and maple. Its main advantage is that access is easier, leaving room for more storage, especially shelves. An added bonus is its function as a dressing room, a much neglected aspect of many hardworking houses that, space permitting, could happily be revived. It is a thoroughly enjoyable luxury to see one's clothes laid out neatly and, at a glance, helps with making decisions when dressing.

lightweight curtains and using light woods such as sycamore, frees the bedroom of built-in furniture. I try to keep built-in cupboards and so on to a minimum because they reduce the apparent size of the architectural envelope, although they are fine if you have a large room. Similarly the American habit of a separate clothes storage room or closet is practical. But the dressing room is a more formal space and determinedly well 'dressed' in the English sense. The provision of such restrained luxury is something for which we might not have enough space, but making use of alcoves as a closet is an option. Otherwise clever use of built-in furniture may be appropriate, if conceived as complementary to the shape and size, proportions, ergonomics and decoration of the room. Otherwise freestanding furniture makes for flexible furnishing and is often my own preference.

CHILDREN'S AND TEENAGERS' ROOMS

Children need their own rooms from around the age of five. Before then privacy isn't important to them – quite the reverse; they need the comforting presence of parents or other siblings. But even by the age of five onwards it feels wrong for children to spend copious amounts of time tucked away in their own rooms. Adults and young children enjoy each other's company and want the reassurance of being within the same vicinity but also require the space to do their own thing. I play with my own children, but mostly I enjoy the spectacle of them playing; likewise they obtain satisfaction from watching adults carry out

Our family skills come together in my daughter Gussie's bedroom. Libby, her grandmother, made the vibrant hand-sewn pelmet, and Lucy Turner, her artist aunt, created the colourful applied frieze on the walls. I designed the room, and Gussie helped paint the walls. The limed oak gives a fresh look.

125

Attic rooms are hard to make use of, especially in the eves. Here Nigel Brown, the furniture maker, and I came up with the idea of wooden Meccano to construct a suspended table on which my son Felix could play with his Lego. When Felix gets older, he might use it as a study/work desk.

some practical task (they don't much like us reading books or newspapers). When we feel the need we can join in with each other's activities. So in our household we don't allocate separate downstairs rooms for children or adults, but we do have rooms that are more dedicated to one or the other.

The living room is geared to adults with slightly more precious furniture, books and antiques. The creative room has plenty of table space and storage, orientated towards children. The furniture there is more robust and casual – bean bags, a large sofa and room to play on the floor. Two long trestle-tables allow the children to leave half-completed projects safe from younger siblings until they are ready to return to them. There are also computer and music facilities but at present no TV; that's in the living room where the adults can control it.

The children's bedrooms are in our case small, and where possible we have tried to encourage them to develop their own furnishing ideas with some guidance. Overdecoration by adults with built-in furniture and rich fabrics can be overwhelming and inflexible and leave little for children to add of themselves. This doesn't preclude guiding them towards some special item of furniture, especially on a small scale. I think they appreciate this, along with secret drawers or the creation of mini-spaces, for example below a bunk bed. Homemade bed covers, toys, furniture, knitted or soft items, curtains, cushions made by Mum and Dad or other relatives always mean a lot to them. As does space to play on the floor and a decent table as well as good natural light, preferably from an eastern aspect to enjoy early morning sun. These are the key design needs for young children's bedrooms.

Teenagers' rooms need more storage and, where possible, extra sound insulation. Soft chairs or bean bags for visitors, bookshelves, good artificial lighting as well as hardworking table tops and floor finishes are vital too. But much of this depends on what workshop or creative space is available elsewhere. During my own childhood I worked in a large old barn with my siblings. We didn't have our own rooms as such, and as a result I never missed this. I had creative space elsewhere, and I enjoyed the company of a large family. Indoors we also had two small living rooms, one for quieter activities, and the other for more sociable activities such as music and games, or just talking.

Teenagers' bedrooms must be practical and flexible enough to cope with a variety of different activities if they are to be useful. At some point the smaller scale furniture of childhood has to go up to the attic, and be replaced by a strong plastic-coated metal garage shelving system and durable wooden furniture. British contemporary designer Alan Brown's furniture, rustic in style and made of solid wood, often without glue, is an enjoyable example of the latter. Bedrooms are preferable for quiet study rather than practical activities. Many houses and apartments don't have enough practical creative space, however, so the bedroom becomes yet another all-purpose flexible room.

Furniture maker Alan Brown designed and made this unusual solid oak furniture with a wax finish for a teenager's cottage bedroom in Wales. Its Hansel and Gretel look gives an eccentric, playful air to the room, which is essentially user-friendly. There is plenty of cupboard and shelf space, a compact desk/study area, and a neutral colour base enhanced by post-box red.

Bathroom

THE history of the bathroom reflects our changing attitude to our bodies. Motives for cleanliness vary over time and depend on ideas connected to the development of science, religion, and technology as well as social conditioning. The earliest models for the modern concept of cleanliness date from Roman times, when bathing was central then to notions of public life. Not until the seventeenth century did cleanliness again become a social issue, this time revived by the Calvinist Christians of the Netherlands. According to Simon Schama, in *The Embarrassment of Riches* (1987), the idea that 'Cleanliness is next to Godliness' was backed by a growing belief in the seventeenth century that what was clean was beautiful.

A refreshing antidote to overdone bathrooms, this illustration by Carl Larsson (1855–1919) reminds me of the simple pleasures associated with bathrooms and the rightness of user-friendly natural materials such as wood and paint in a bathroom. It's a relaxing space in which to wash away the cares of the world and enjoy a luxurious soak.

In the eighteenth century, presentation – personal appearance, tidiness, and elegance – became an obsession of polite society; nevertheless, the practice of regular bathing was uncommon. A return visit to those times would strike most of us on an olfactory level as one of the most arresting differences in daily life between then and now. It all seems alien to our present standards of cleanliness, and sometimes I wonder if we haven't gone too far the other way, not so much in terms of bodily washing but in our attitudes to newness and purity, the sense of being untouchable, overclean and disconnected.

Once advances in medicine early in the nineteenth century began to prove that disease stemmed from the spread of germs, this combined with other social forces to develop planned sewerage and water supply systems. This was clearly a necessity for survival, especially after serious outbreaks of cholera, a bacterial disease spread through infected water. It focused public concern to the point where, by the 1920s, every middle-class residence had their own bathroom. But, even as late as the 1960s, some working-class homes in England were still not fully plumbed. Victorian prejudice had lingered, along with poverty.

For those of us who have a choice, the bathroom is now a social room. Steam chambers and high-pressure showers with oil-scented candlelit baths, perfumed soap, soft towels and an easy chair are what we expect of today's bathroom. So, too, are exquisite marble slabs and finishes, shiny tiles and well-sculpted white porcelain basins and appliances, subtle white brass fittings, cast-iron baths and elegant mirrors. Gone is the era of the apologetic bathroom. The day of something more sensuous has arrived, and the technical back-up is now formidable.

The view from the tiny bathroom window is a church spire. Sadly, too many contemporary bathrooms are windowless, so whenever I design a bathroom I try to place the bath next to a window; or, as in this case, for a house in Gloucestershire, I built a window right next to the bath with flared sides for maximum visibility.

BELOW
An alternative bathroom sink cabinet design which provides storage in the curved apron-fronted base and a tapering eye level cupboard that allows easier access to the sink bowl as it continues leftwards.

RIGHT
The palette of materials in a bathroom is mostly restricted to those that are water-tolerant. Here I have proposed among others, Portuguese limestone non-porous floor slabs, a one-piece, curved marble bath panel, handmade wall tiles, a stainless-steel structure for the sink cabinet and lacquered cherrywood, wherever there is intermittent contact with water and gloss paint. The stool was to be made in an oiled hardwood.

Steam rooms, pressurized shower performance and delivery of hot water with serious extraction of steam mean that there is tremendous wear and tear on the bathroom's internal fabric and wall finishes. And yet many of us feel that it should feel less like a Turkish bath and more like a furnished room. Wooden floors, preferably with a Persian rug, are commonly requested by my clients, although an unsuitable proposition in many cases. How to resolve all this is a challenge, especially as the bathroom is nearly always chosen because it is either small or has an awkward shape. It is often the room of the house that can't be used for anything else. For a shower room or WC combination, that's fine. For a bathroom, it's not.

The bathroom also makes the most technical demands of any household room: water causes serious damage if it is allowed to drip unwanted on to surfaces or to seep undetected into nooks and crannies. Damp is an enemy of the householder and in all rooms, except the kitchen, is exiled internally. Controlling the effects of water in the bathroom is tricky but vital.

There is some suggestion that bathrooms might become fitness centres or mini-gyms, but this requires a lot of space, and water, ever present in bathrooms, would damage many keep-fit appliances. Nevertheless I can see a move towards the bathroom becoming a more sociable room. The shower is taking over from the bath as the most common form of daily washing, with bathing now an evening luxury, pep-me-up – or, more probably, calm-me-down. But why not turn it into an event to be shared, as the Japanese do? Bathing in Japan is a social activity. Some European families do have baths together, particularly parents with young children. Why not extend this to reading books, listening to music or drinking a glass of wine? It's a good way of doubling-up on relaxation. Situating the bath near a window with a wonderful view also adds quality to the bathing experience. I can recommend it.

THE MODERN FAMILY BATHROOM

Quietly modern but with an efficient shower and sociable double-ended bath for young children and an available parent to enjoy was the basis of the brief for this project. The floor, made from an impervious, warm-coloured Portuguese limestone, was designed to link in with the shower, so excess water could be drained off. By setting the shower floor 25mm (1in) below the main floor of the bathroom and fitting a glass screen on the third side, some 95 per cent of the water stays within the shower area. The continuous limestone floor obviates the need for a shower door, making the shower area look more open and friendly. The generous pale marble bath surround provides plenty of putting-down space, another welcoming feature. There was an attempt to ensure that all the materials we used should appear as soft and sensual as possible in order to offset the coldness of the surfaces of the many waterproof materials – marble, glass, stainless steel and porcelain. The marble bath panel was carved into an elongated S-shaped profile, and the screen surround is acid-etched with a large wavy pattern so as to appear softer and more subtly textured. The Portuguese limestone floor was chosen for its warm natural colour, texture and appearance, as was the pink Rose Aurora

ABOVE
View of the doorless walk-in shower. By laying the whole floor with water-resistant material and sloping it carefully there is no need for an enclosing door. The shower floor is set slightly below the main floor to retain as much water as possible. The remainder gently flows back towards it. Among the benefits is good visibility of the view across the fields.

LEFT
The virtues of the unfitted bathroom. Freestanding, characterful individual elements are used wherever possible, rather than built-in cupboards, showers and 'alcoves'. They create a more spacious appearance and allow the architecture of the room to enjoy a clearer expression. Everything is exposed, although the view from the window is discreet.

BELOW
By making the stainless-steel wash basin freestanding, light can permeate all around it so it presents no barrier to light levels in the room. The windowsill is linked to the height of the bath, permitting a wonderful view from the tub (although in more over-looked areas it might be necessary to use etched or opaque glass that still permits shapes, but ensures total privacy).

RIGHT
The roll-top edge in Rosa Aurora marble acts as both a handle for leverage and a footrest while towel-drying your legs. It also softens the square edge, so climbing into the bath becomes more pleasant. The double-ended bath means that bathing can be enjoyed by more than one person at a time.

marble roll on the bath edge. This marble can withstand being turned on a lathe, and the rim of the bath doubles as a handle for getting in and out of the bath more easily and a footrest for drying your feet once you are out of it.

The handmade stainless-steel basin was specially shaped to sit unobtrusively round the window recess. The window itself was widened and lowered to afford a view across the garden from the luxury of a warm bath. Finally to avoid any chance of flooding or damp travelling into the rooms downstairs, the whole room was tanked with fibreglass up to a height of just over half a metre (2ft) before the floor was laid, something I now recommend as standard. I also installed a pump to increase the water pressure and put an end to all those jokes about English showers.

THE ATTIC BATHROOM

This is where bathrooms often end up. On this occasion we had a decent length of room with which to work, although it was only possible to stand up at the centre of the attic. The bath was set on a step at the end of the room and nestled in tightly between two side cupboards. The delicate nature of the design, particularly of the towel racks and panelling, counteracted the imposing effect of the roof in the room and focused the eye at a lower level, which was particularly enjoyable when actually bathing. The attic window overlooked the countryside, offered stunning views and was incorporated positively into the overall design.

Bathrooms often end up consigned to the attic or left-over spaces. This illustration shows one way of using the eves to best advantage, thus minimizing the corridor effect caused by the length of the room. The sunlight-on-water paint patterns were inspired by David Hockney's series of Los Angeles pool paintings.

I have long been an admirer of artist David Hockney's paintings, especially his ability to reinvent depictions of water. His series of paintings of the pool at his Los Angeles home is remarkable. His water patterns have altered the way we look at water and expanded our visual language. His work on opera sets also brilliantly shows off his skill at creating artificial surface and highly original, decorative paint effects. In this bathroom design I tried, with Richard Lee, the contemporary British visual artist, to adapt Hockney's ideas into a more formal paint effect to act as a kind of visual appetizer or accompaniment to the process of bathing.

Missing Rooms

HOME OFFICE

Working at home has so many advantages that I can't think why big business has taken so long to latch on to them. Admittedly the advent of fax machines and computers make it much easier today than ever before. When the factory system was introduced in late eighteenth-century Britain, studies reveal that it was accompanied by a decrease in productivity, for example, in the weaving industry. Such cottage industries – the precursors and ongoing alternatives to the large-scale factory system – were popular, flexible and humane, motivating each individual and extending the psychological security blanket of home, with its feelings of familiarity, safety and comfort, to the workplace. In fact this world of work did not have the separation from home activities that

The workroom in artist Carl Larsson's home in 1909 includes a spinning wheel, a hand-weaving loom, a vast multi-purpose table/desk and house space for his children. The idea of one room where all the family can work together seems thoroughly civilized and practical.

it has today; it was, after all, merely another survival activity, like cooking, fetching firewood or making candles. Grouping people together in offices or factories allows only an external control; it is not possible to change their inner motivation or improve their concentration, both of which, in my view, perk up in a benevolent environment.

Many of us who work at home can do so quite happily at the kitchen table, which says a lot about the benefits of the home environment. But for those who need specialist equipment, space for storage, ready access to books or plenty of room to manoeuvre, then clearly a dedicated room is required – certainly for part of the time not least because of the necessary separation from family activity. Distractions at home are among the main reasons, along with motivation or self-discipline, that are cited as objections to working there.

Self-discipline is partly a matter of habit and will be a short-lived problem, providing that your work is to your liking. Being away from family activity is more of a sound (or sight) problem, especially if you have children. A separate building, such as a garden shed, seems ideal, likewise an attic or a room that is outside the main domestic-activity zone. My children get used to my working presence in the house. They can come into my studio (I have always worked at home), but they know I am a little boring there, so after saying hello they tend to disappear. Sometimes, especially in the latter part of the day, they join me to do paperwork – drawing or artwork – which is normally not too disturbing.

We all like this arrangement. They pick up concentration from you; if not they can move on. I think it good, where appropriate, for children to see parents at work. My father had his doctor's surgery at home in the afternoons, and we used to chat to the patients. It made the atmosphere more relaxed for them, and we learnt something about his work and dealing with unfamiliar adults, as well as being able to see our father between patients.

Artists and writers often worked at home with private space available for their creative expression, among them the turn-of-the-century Swedish watercolourist, illustrator and history painter, Carl Larsson, whose studio space is illustrated opposite. His room is unusual because it appears to have been shared with his family, which is rare as most artists need quiet space for intense concentration. But the creative process does require variable degrees of attention at different stages, and clearly Larsson realized this. I suspect there are a great many other unrecognized 'creative' workers at home who practise just such a way of life, sometimes enjoying the company of other people while working.

The communication advantages today, with the new information technology, allow for many business activities to be carried out at home. The trend will surely increase, so that new houses will begin to incorporate a work space. But it is equally possible and worthwhile to create a home office in older houses, where necessity is often the mother of invention. Working at home can make better use of your house, and by cutting down travel time, it gives you more opportunity to enjoy your home.

How to squeeze in a home–office space from the small landing of a flat. Cleverly designed by Jeremy Melvin by using light and elegant materials, the airy and apparently capacious result belies its cramped circumstances. This is clearly a working rather than a sociable environment, a self-contained work zone that is part of, yet crucially apart from, the relaxed environment of the living room.

135

MUSIC ROOM

Making music used to be an integral part of home entertainment. Historically, music rooms were sociable places for evening or family get-togethers. There was no need for soundproofing, although professional musicians practising at home must have caused some disturbance to their respective households. By the eighteenth century most grand houses made some provision for music as part of the activities of civilized life. Since there was no recorded music, it had to be self-generated, making it somehow more precious and eagerly anticipated. Prior to this musicians would often travel the country together in small groups, visiting grand houses for short periods to provide music for special family occasions or local festivals.

Without TVs and stereo systems musical gatherings were one way of giving family life purpose and direction, of encouraging sociability in the evenings. Today we are lucky if the piano is played at all, for far fewer of us than ever seem to learn it – and musical evenings are a rarity. Recently I was asked by British rock musician Howard Jones to create a room where he could make music professionally but in a domestic environment. He wanted a space not only where the process of music-making could be deinstitutionalized but also to provide somewhere his family could use in the evenings and at weekends as a 'media', music and entertainments room. The whole project was made enjoyable by the Jones's enthusiasm and input as well as the idiosyncrasy and size of the space. Planned in four zones, the efficiency of the working environment

Planned around four key activities, this view shows Howard Jones's rise-and-fall keyboard console that can be used either seated or standing up for performance. On the right is the recording desk. Cables fit under the grill-covered channel near the perimeter. All the music equipment is treated like furniture and can be dismantled to take on tour.

was domesticated and enhanced by the comfort element of a seating area. In one of the zones is the giant grand piano. When visiting musicians wish to play, the sofa and armchairs are moved out of the way to clear a performance area.

Recording studios have become sterile places concerned with 'dead' spaces, where acoustics are flat or non-responsive. Many musicians today have recording studios at home. This is feasible now because the obsession with very loud music has subsided along with the recognition that it can cause hearing damage, and soundproofing techniques have improved too. Triple glazing, soundproofing materials and the development of acoustic engineering techniques for large public auditoria, such as opera houses and theatres, mean that noise disturbance is less and so containable within domestic premises. Thus recording music does not need to be done at specially constructed studios. In addition, computerized music systems give a lot more flexibility to make music without resorting to large orchestras, which all means that the home environment can accommodate recording requirements more easily.

Brian Eno, the well-known musician and record producer, is one of the thinkers and movers behind trying to take recording techniques into a new dimension, to emphasize the use of natural or 'live' spaces in which to record. Eno says this helps make for more interesting music with a live-performance feel to it. The environment I have designed here with Howard Jones's guidance backs this up and, I hope, sets a precedent for intermingling our domestic life more with our working environment. It has a civilizing influence, and mixes both modern and traditional design at the same time. If this can happen anywhere, it should be in the world of music.

This view shows the seating area. A huge pull-down TV/video/ home-movie screen descends from the chequerboard panel situated at the top of the cupboard on the left. The cupboard itself stores five keyboards and a variety of musical instruments and paraphernalia. To retain an at-home atmosphere and to deaden the acoustics, specially designed carpets by Lucy Turner were to be commissioned to help delineate and domesticate each zone of activity except for the area around the grand piano.

137

MEDIA ROOM

With the increasing sophistication of TV and music systems, the 'Home Theatre' concept – a fully insulated, dedicated room – is an aid to privacy. Noise pollution from efficient stereo and surround-sound systems is a new but growing problem. Loud music or television talk that leaks into other rooms is invasive. The only way to avoid it is by dedicating separate rooms to watching television or listening to music that can be effectively closed off from the rest of the house. I suspect that any remaining notion that fully open-plan houses are desirable for families is over. Large spaces are wonderful, but sound is so intrusive that they are only enjoyable if TV and music can be enclosed in a separate soundproof 'box'.

I have recently been designing both individual pieces of furniture and entire media rooms. Surround-sound need speakers placed in special positions. Attractive new control systems, for example by the Danish hi-fi company Bang & Olufsen, make their technology worthy of display. Their fine detailing, futuristic use of design and high-quality craftsmanship complement furniture and add excitement to the interior. Adding big sofas, soft floors, controlled lighting and fireplaces wherever possible creates a predominantly night-time

The subtle curve in the plan of the giant media cupboard offsets the rigidity of the grid. Perversely it also provides the flexibility needed for the placement of the speakers at the precise points required by surround-sound systems. The giant scale of the moulding around the screen draws the eye away from its size.

The entrance to the media room is designed as a domestic space. This domestication of 'professional', or office, interiors makes them more friendly and relaxing. This design, in the house of a well-known broadcaster, had to serve for both family and business use. There is space for the fax machine, phone, books and storage, all in a relaxing environment.

BOTTOM LEFT
The raised-height fireplace gives it more visibility. The tall, curved cabinet houses stereo equipment and acts as a heat shield for the television screen.

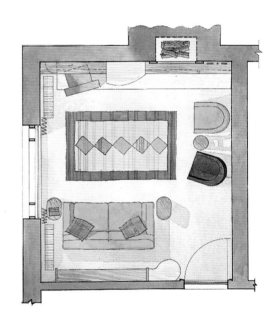

ABOVE
The restrictions inherent in the relationship between television and fireplace are often a problem in determining the position of a seating circle. With this plan there is a simple, traditional layout as both are adjacent.

atmosphere, in which snugness, cosiness and separateness from the outside world allows the viewers to escape fully. The media room is a cross between a private cinema, a library and a living room. All these rooms had a great pedigree, but contained together in a contemporary way with soundproofing the media room provides a comfortable and practical model for the future.

RIGHT AND BELOW
A giant TV screen needs subduing. One effective way of ensuring this is to house it within a substantial moulding and a roller-shutter. Here I have designed a picture frame to enclose and contain it. The scale of the surroundings and various adjacent pieces of furniture helps – the generous sofa, well set back, and the intimacy of the space – as does the scale provided by the grid.

THE CREATIVE ROOM/WORKSHOP

The opportunity for creativity and provision of suitable environments to facilitate this is, in my opinion, one of the major functions of the home. For those of us who go out to work during the week, it can be activity at the weekend that helps keep us sane; for those at home all the time, it is vital.

So many rooms, especially overdecorated ones, restrict us to social activity. Why does a workshop have to be outside in a separate building? It doesn't, unless the space it needs has some special requirement, such as a particular height, an extra-large doorway or noise insulation; usually it's located externally because of shortage of room internally. But rooms where hobbies are carried out are often looked down upon, although, as indicated by George Santayana in his *Soliloquy on the British Character* (*c.*1880), 'England is the paradise of individuality, eccentricity, heresy, anomalies, hobbies and humours.'

Are our hobbies better conducted outside the house? Domestic activities, especially the feminine ones, have always been carried on inside it, because they were less obtrusive; children's ones confined to nurseries and the rest of them to potting sheds. Many of our creative outlets are simply just denied or frustrated by lack of suitable space. Ironically, it is that room already overcrowded with uses, the kitchen, that often ends up including a surrogate workshop among its multifarious roles, especially for children. A soundproofed place for music, and media enjoyment, for meditation or solitude, a room to catch winter sun, a cool place that moderates the summer heat, all have their place; a large kitchen central to them all is, as I described in *The Art of Kitchen Design* (1994), vital, but a workshop or series of practical creative spaces seems the most common thing missing in homes of today.

Hours spent in creative activity, where time gets forgotten, release the mind from the burdens of everyday life. This renews our spirits and encourages our vitality. Spending time playing and fiddling about with often obscure projects can leave us with an insatiable desire to design, make and create. How many children, brought up in small city apartments, could benefit from the tremendous confidence gained from making toys or furniture, restoring carts or building land yachts, I wonder? Attics, cellars and potting sheds have great potential for this, and even kitchens – the creative centre of last resort. Ironically the least sophisticated rooms are often the most used. Time, money and thought is always spent on the grander rooms – the front room parlour, or the dining room – which are occupied less.

It is frequently the abstract or non-physical element of rooms that we recall with greatest relish. The views out of the window can give so much atmosphere. The shape of the room is vital, too, especially if it is in an attic, where the power of the roof is transmitted into the space. In the end the activity carried out in any room makes an impact there; rooms where creative work is accomplished must leave us with some of our strongest associations – with the possible exception of our connections with the hearth. Fires usually spark off memories, associations and desire for reflection, but so does our creative life.

A room for hobbies. Many rooms restrict us to social activities or non-practical uses. A workshop or creative room is important for adults, as well as children. A place to make a creative mess is vital for every one of us. Often our most memorable rooms from childhood are those where creativity was possible – rather than soft furnishings!

What is the essence of a good workshop? Good tools, storage in a variety of forms, plenty of bench-top space, preferably at different heights, ample floor room, tall ceilings and the opportunity to make noise and mess and leave work in progress undisturbed are all vital. Access to natural light is important, too, if long periods of time are spent there, while access to the outside in the form of a flat, hard surface into which to extend during clement weather is extremely advantageous.

Whether being shown around a friend's home workshop or visiting a craftsman's workspace, I feel a tremendous excitement. It is like a vacuum of opportunity, pregnant with possibility. I can't quantify how a workshop space can contribute to our lives – and how it did to mine. But I am sure an opportunity to use this wonderful work/play zone can make a big difference to our efficiency and enjoyment.

The lack of opportunity today for adults and children to experiment and to make things in a workshop space at home contributes to delinquency, crime and possibly depression. Equally, one of the least salutary aspects of the success of mass consumer culture and the use of low-wage third-world labour is the widespread availability of cheaply made household goods and its subsequent undermining of the homemade, from Christmas decorations to basic wooden shelves or cushion covers. Another unfortunate corollary of modern manufacturing techniques is the need for efficiency's sake to split the making process into narrow bands of activity that de-skill the capacity of the maker or operative, so as to be useless outside of a production line. It is, for example, like training a chairmaker only to turn the legs or to make the seats, the backs or arms. De-skilling is a real problem today with consequences for our personal lives. One way to combat it is to take on the role of a confident amateur and plunge in with a kind of mad courage and determination in our home lives.

The tremendous success of housewife superstar Martha Stewart's home show series on American television and of her monthly magazine is founded on giving people the confidence to go out and make things for themselves through demonstrating the techniques in easy stages and by inspiring them with the end-results. Although her initial emphasis was on home cooking, her more recent programmes demonstrate practical activities from home improvements to tent-making. Her shows are popular partly because they stir up innate but dominant instincts of creativity that we all harbour.

Workshops aren't the only places where creativity takes place or is possible, but they are venues where there is both a sense of freedom from sociable invasion and an invitation to experiment, make a noise and some mess with a repository for tools etc. All of this encourages our creativity, and in the end that is what matters.

The light flooding in from the floor-to-ceiling windows and the well-ordered tool racks of this indoor workshop suggest an immediate opportunity for getting down to something creative.

Conservatory or Garden Room

The domestic conservatory started off life as a 'fashion accessory' to grander homes and was more a place to take tea and deport oneself socially, rather than for housing exotic plants. In this mid-nineteenth-century painting The Rivals *by James Jacques Joseph Tissot (1836–1902) the plants were kept more appropriately in a separate chamber, visible through glass.*

THE origin of the word conservatory comes from the name for a place where things are kept safe and conserved, providing especially a means of shelter for exotic or young plants, as in a greenhouse. In Italy a conservatory was originally a hospital for foundlings, such as the Pio Ospedale della Pietà in Venice, where Vivaldi nurtured young musical talent, and children were 'conserved' to become useful citizens. The conservatoire also exists in France in a similar sense. Its history in Britain is different. Sir Joseph Paxton, the nineteenth-century English gardener and architect, was head gardener to the Duke of Devonshire at Chiswick and Chatsworth, where he remodelled the gardens and built the lily house and conservatory (1840s), revolutionary buildings with prefabricated sections of cast-iron and glass. Prince Albert, Queen Victoria's consort, realized their potential and proposed a massive version to house the world's first International Trade exhibition. In 1851, at London's Hyde Park, up to 24,000 people a day visited this extraordinary apparition, nicknamed the 'Crystal Palace', at the Great Exhibition.

The technology today is a little more sophisticated in its use of glass and steel, but in the nineteenth century this innovative transparent structure had a profound effect on Victorian public buildings, resulting in work of tremendous beauty, particularly at Kew Botanical Gardens. It was used extensively in London and for public buildings, especially railway stations. On a private scale the conservatory became fashionable not only as a place to grow exotic plants that a northern climate could not otherwise nurture but also as somewhere to enjoy the sun on windy days and provide a pleasant location to converse and have fun with family and friends.

Due to the high level of moisture needed to encourage the growth of plants, durable consrtruction materials had to be used. This meant that although the greenery softened the overall atmosphere, they were not rooms to dwell in too long. This has changed in recent years because our yearning for exotic plants has been facilitated by the introduction of environmental growth techniques. Now underfloor heating, double or even triple, glazing, sophisticated and auto-mated blind/sun-control systems make them suitable for use as dining rooms, extended kitchens and living rooms.

A key difference between our modern twentieth-century houses and their predecessors is in our ability to control light. We have the technology not

BELOW
Here a conservatory links the kitchen into a walled garden. My clients commissioned the stone-carver Richard Podd to make the exotic carving of an elephant; the dog (above) was created by Ben Harms and Raymond Gonzales of G & H Studios, Somerset.

The conservatory is large enough to provide a seating area and a carpet on which children can play. The heat gain is minimized by blinds and by making part of the roof opaque. Too much glass can be unwelcome in extremes of weather and temperature.

only to make glasswork to deal with heat loss and gain but also to control light levels. Manipulation and use of light is a major component of good design and one of the key innovations of modern architecture that differentiates old from new houses. Old buildings tend to be darker with smaller windows and, for historically understandable reasons, less open to the outside. One obvious way to redress the light balance in an older house is to add a conservatory. This can also provide an additional room in the house that can release space for other activities. The conservatory is also a particularly useful

way of linking the house to the garden. In the conservatory pictured here it does all those jobs at once – and more. It provides a dining room, with the old dining room now a study–library. It connects the kitchen to the court-yard garden and refocuses the house to its southern aspect. It brings light and warmth into the hall and kitchen. There is also considerable heat gain from a conservatory, which can be reabsorbed by the rest of the house. Alternative energy consultants now realize the importance of this for energy-efficient houses in northern climates.

The inside of the Gloucestershire conservatory shown on the previous page. In planning terms it takes pressure off the kitchen and allows for a generous eating table, an informal relaxation area and a place for children to play. It also conveniently links up the kitchen to the walled garden.

The conservatory has a different quality to other rooms because of its exposure to the weather and the amount of light it gets. In some ways it is an outdoor, or garden, room with transparent walls. Traditionally, it was popular and expedient to grow exotic plants here that could not otherwise be grown in northern climates, thus turning it into a 'nature' room. The impact of so much greenery raised moisture levels and meant that furniture had to be made of water-resistant durable materials, hence the use of cast-iron tables and planters, cane and willow chairs. Today the sun room or conservatory is used more as casual dining space or as a low-key and relaxing outdoors living room. As sun deprivation is now recognized as a problem (known as SAD – seasonal affective disorder), causing depression for those of us in northern climates, it is a real advantage to have a 'sun' room.

There are problems of weather control to be surmounted, however, or the conservatory–sun room can become a bleak place in winter and, conversely, intolerably hot in summer. Originally they were not rooms in which to dwell too long. Today underfloor heating is advisable, or at least radiators sunk below floor-level with cathedral grills over them to cope with the winter cold. But the large quantities of glass required call for the serious use of blinds or curtains. On the roof, blinds are needed to cope with UV-light damage, and the only non-synthetic material I can recommend is some kind of natural fabric made from either cane or reeds. For the walls, where sun damage will be less harsh, except in Australia and other sun-drenched climes, then fabric blinds are fine, and wooden- or metal-slatted blinds are ideal. Either way keeping out the image of winter cold is psychologically comforting. In summer, filtering the light is essential, and that is where slatted blinds come into their own. Glen Murcutt, the Australian architect, recommends putting blinds on the outside in hot climates so as to minimize heat penetration in the first place. The roof is the place where the filtration of light is most regularly in need of control. Motorized blinds help here, because we are more likely to use them. Sometimes half-glazing the roof is helpful. Nearby trees that provide semi-shade are a bonus.

This may sound complicated but having one room in the house that is more closely connected to the world outside than the rest of the house is surely an asset. It is a space we can use with great pleasure that extends the period of the year during which we can enjoy our gardens – right from early spring into the late autumn – protecting us from wind and inclement weather. Fitted with generous French doors, it allows us to enjoy the garden at times when we couldn't sit outside even during the summer. By indulging in some external lighting, we can also extend the pleasures of garden viewing into the evening.

A room with a view – of 20 miles of countryside – in this first-floor conservatory, which has the atmosphere of a colonial clubhouse without its drawbacks. The flip-top table doubles as both a dining and billiards table. The chairs will have detachable, slip-on covers, appropriate for summer and winter use. Effective light control is obviously essential, but the blinds had yet to be chosen when this drawing was carried out. A substantial cabinet (not in picture) houses a music system.

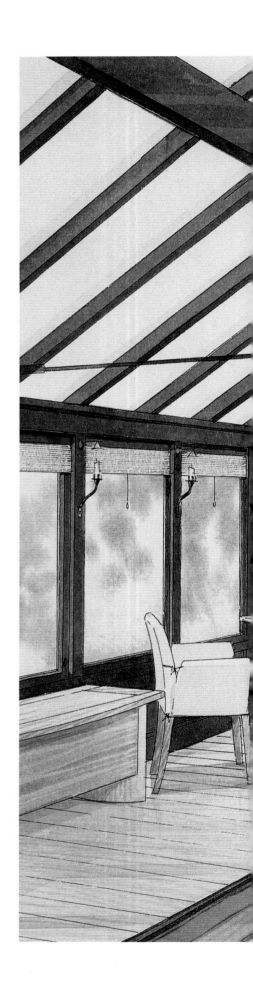

FIVE
CONTEMPORARY
DESIGNERS'
SOLUTIONS

The view into the stairwell at the Lawson–Westen House designed by Eric Owen Moss which illustrates the originality and sense of surprise created by his geometry.

Introduction

Architects and designers are necessary for the production of sophisticated buildings – ones that work well and are aesthetically pleasing. I have selected five highly-regarded professionals: two from the UK, Charles Rutherfoord (above) and Christopher Nevile; one from Australia, Glen Murcutt (below opposite); two from the USA, Eric Owen Moss and Arquitectonica (above opposite). All of them have talents that go beyond mere technical skill. They have that added ingredient – an understanding of what gives a space a sense of poetry and makes a rational assembly of materials, ideas and craftsmanship into a humane, enticing and wholesome environment.

A hardworking house implies one that can be well used; that is capable of performance. The array of technology available to make a house work is truly awesome; not just in the bolt-on technology of machines but in the live performance of the building skin as well. We humans have woven around this nesting instinct of ours such a sophisticated web of possibility that few, if any, of us can have access to all the knowledge and skills available. The home remains a major focus of our industrial and commercial civilization; tremendous resources are poured into it every year, and for many of us it remains the major comforting and cohesive element not only in our personal and family life but for society too.

The best way to make sense of this array of technological choice is by employing expert assistance. The first stage to any project has to be to set up a brief, that is to lay the 'thinking' foundation in order to get the 'design' right. Design really means the 'thinking' part. Does anybody need trained designers to help design their home? Yes, we all do to some extent, assuming that resources are available. Unless there is personal knowledge of the project by the client, it is advisable, even if only in preliminary stages.

Design assistance to home owners comes essentially from three professional groups: from architects for the outside and for assistance with its relation to the inside; from interior designers for the interior planning and specification; and from interior decorators for the softer elements, such as fabrics, upholstery, furniture and accessories. Ideally it would be good if all these skills could be found in one person, but in practice this is extremely rare and perhaps too all encompassing for anyone.

Architects are vital for large-scale construction works and new houses because they are trained to understand the cultural and spatial concepts of a building structure in a way that surveyors and engineers are not. They are taught to think broadly and about how to coordinate with other skills. It is vital to understand and develop a real sensitivity for interior space and the minutiae of activities that go on there, and this is something by and large best left to interior designers who are happier working on a smaller scale. This is especially so in hardworking areas such as the kitchen, bathroom or the multiuse media room. There are exceptions, of course. Some architects have understood and implemented designs at this level because of personal interest. For a while I have been operating under the title Interior Architect, which combines architectural and interior-design skills, and I would dearly love to reorganize the design professions to create this new category with an academic back-up, especially with an accent on domestic design. This is overdue and will occur, I suspect, over the next decade for the householder is poorly served by the design profession at present, with commerce and industry its main orientation.

For me, like many other designers, the pleasure involved in solving a small-scale design problem, is tremendously satisfying. All my imaginative powers are drawn on; knowledge of material, the appropriate craftspeople and machinery available. I investigate innovatory forms and shapes, new combinations of material and construction, research historical ideas and detail subtle changes to link up a variety of cultural references. I make abstract judgements, such as the feature's overall impact in the space, its friendliness or intended 'poetic' quality – surprise, delight, visual weight, texture or colour. Finally, I look at how well it copes with its intended basic function: will it keep the water out? Can it be used on more than one bath panel?

I am not saying that design can always bring obvious and easy joys. On many occasions its function is more mundane. Anyone who has had agonizing discussions about the type of sink to use in the kitchen, or what colour to paint the wall can vouch for this. But good design can be a real benefit to the way we use, and how much we enjoy, our own domestic environment. If this sounds like an advertisement for interior designers, then it is. Certainly, time to think about the design is vital before any project begins, especially before employing a designer. The much used aphorism – 'a good patron always gets a good project' – is so true. A well thought-out brief starts in motion a distinct and clear decision-making process.

There is a genuine worry among all potential house restorers, rebuilders or refurbishers when about to employ an architect or designer: will the professionals take over the project and diminish their own role in the process? This is an age-old problem. And it is a fascinating dilemma for the designer, who must listen, guide and propose, and help to obtain the right balance.

In the end the professionals selected must be people the home owners can trust and with whom they can feel comfortable. The designer should question the brief in order to do their job properly. Likewise, the designer should propose at least some innovations, or there might be some doubt about what they are going to give to the project. So client, I beseech you, give your designer some lattitude – at least at the early stages when brainstorming will benefit the range and depth of possibility. And designers, I beg of you, please listen very closely to both the emotional and psychological as well as the practical needs of the client. Equally, as I said in *The Art of Kitchen Design,* we should draw on our intuition.

My initial decision to select five influential contemporary designers from the wealth of talent that exists today seemed virtually impossible to achieve. But eventually I decided not simply to focus on proven design skills but to give equal emphasis to the attitudes and ideas behind the work. All five of them have a capacity to express their vision with tremendous clarity, sense of purpose and mastery of technical skill, combined with the ability to communicate visual delight and poetic quality more than simply knowing how to solve technical problems. I have tried to elucidate the key qualities that make my chosen designers special, and to show how much value their ideas have for us and how they fit into the core ideas behind this book.

Glen Murcutt:
The Poetry of Modernism

ABOVE

Sunset view of Magney House (1984), Bingey Point, NSW, Australia. The simple beauty of this house standing in an isolated beach in mid-New South Wales resolves many of the ambiguities in modern building. Decisions taken with a firm hand, using advance technological skill, produce a quietude that escapes the fussiness and disorder found in so many contemporaneous buildings.

RIGHT

Control of the external environment, particularly light and air movement, without resorting to expensive air-conditioning is one of Murcutt's key interests. There is a quality of calmness or understated design that allows for a sense of repose.

B Y the early eighties there were many who thought that Modernism's days were numbered. Its failures were common knowledge and its buildings unpopular: inhuman tower blocks, ugly office buildings and factories; characterless, dreary and soul-less city centres. But during the last 20 years Australian architect and designer Glen Murcutt (*b* 1936) never tired of his faith in Modern Movement core ideas, and viewed from this point (1996) his belief is justified. The revival, not just survival, of Modernism generally is now self-evident. The reasons for its inadequacies are clearer now. Modernism nevertheless shows an unexpected tenacity and seems to be able to claim a durability as the predominant mentality of the intellectual élite at the end of the twentieth century.

Glen Murcutt, in my opinion, is an architect/designer who has reinterpreted Modernism and has given back not only its earlier lost promise but also a new and distinctly humane orientation. He combines his sense of modernity with an understanding of place rooted in the Australian vernacular. Ironically, Murcutt's work helped to revive Australian vernacular architecture

through his use of corrugated-iron roofs, simple timber construction with weather-boarding timber blinds and giant water-storage tanks that have become accepted parts of his language. With his Modernist sense of space he infuses into these traditions some thoroughly new thinking. His designs for main rooms are often large and airy, appropriate to their function with careful control of light and air movement and a flexible response to aspect and climate. He uses hardworking surfaces and, on the outside in particular, plans for the effects of age. He also prefers natural materials, local where possible, as in the Arts and Crafts tradition.

Murcutt considers his chief influences as the leader of the purist school of Modern architecture, the German-born architect Mies van der Rohe – with his Farnsworth House (1950), Chicago – and Pierre Chareau – with his Maison de Verre (1931), Paris. The former is the ultimate logical expression of building enclosure put before domestic comfort; the latter, to quote Murcutt, 'Modernism without dogma', a celebration of craft and industry working together. As an architect he is driven by a sensitive and sophisticated philosophy and a great love of Australia. The unthinking application of European cultural values into Australian life has caused massive ugliness there, engendering alienation from the landscape and a feeling of discomfort in a misfit, disconnected culture. Glen Murcutt is one of the pioneers among writers, artists and conservationists responsible for trying to raise consciousness about how nature and landscape are endangered by both big business and private interests. His work counters all this by creating spaces, houses and places that really fit into the landscape, making his clients feel literally at home in Australia.

I believe Murcutt's intensive study of nature has loosened him from the orthodoxies of Modernism and enabled him to be more humane, more connected to and inspired by the places where his buildings are sited, as can be seen, for example, at Magney House (1984), Bingey Point, NSW. It has encouraged him to develop an architectural language for the Australian house. His acceptance of the harsh climate means that he works with nature, not against it. He avoids energy-intensive air-conditioning by designing with care, for example, louvred glass walls. Winter sunlight penetrates his buildings through strategically angled wooden slats above skylights, while summer sunlight is kept outside, with the assistance of external blinds. Traditional verandas are avoided because they create dark areas in the rooms behind them and increase heat levels by slowing down or trapping the movement of air, especially at the higher ceiling level.

In the Ball–Eastaway House (1983), he attaches great importance to outside rooms. At one end of the house is a large covered deck that is effectively an outside room. There is also a smaller, rectangular niche taken out of the north-west elevation, designed as a meditation deck. This has a flat ceiling so that no hot air is trapped at the top, and with no railing to spoil the sightline (when seated) nature can be contemplated unhindered. The building, which stands on stilts, is in some sense no more than a large and sophisticated mobile home; the surrounding landscape is left totally undisturbed.

Meagher House (1988, external view NSW, Australia). Murcutt's recent work uses more solid frames and masonry. His abiding interest lies in how to link buildings with the landscape. With this in mind he has extended the house through outdoor rooms. These frame views from the inside, as well as acting as an environmental filter and creating a private enclosure with the opportunity to have a formalized garden area.

LEFT
The Ball–Eastaway House (1983), Mangrove Mountain, NSW. Clear, uncluttered spaces with character, light and a sense of order. This shows the open plan design with the kitchen on the right and the freestanding fireplace on the other side. The curved ceiling creates a feeling of spaciousness, additional height where needed and a strong link to metal-engineered structures.

BELOW
Murcutt's belief is for buildings to tread 'lightly on the earth'. The Ball–Eastaway House stands on stilts so the bush is left untouched. It is wittily suggestive of a mobile home, gypsy caravan or even a railway carriage, especially with its cross-section and curved roof.

It's a sound philosophy – buildings should tread lightly on the natural landscape, and we need to formulate our way of life more in harmony with nature. Many visionaries have said this – Henry David Thoreau, Mahatma Ghandi, Rachel Carson and E. F. Schumacher among others – as well as innumerable contemporary environmentalists. In the Ball–Eastaway House and many of his other buildings Glen Murcutt has shown how it can be done. His designs have a sense of quietism that avoids acts of self-consciousness and eschews the visual gestures often used to liven up otherwise dull architecture. His interiors are not only rationally planned but also contain a feeling of generosity combined with the craftsmanship and a cool, restrained use of invention. This leaves the insides of his buildings as oases of calm rather than the hot-house, oppressive atmosphere of overdesigned interiors.

Now that one-off houses are commissioned with increasing rarity, especially in Britain, it is perhaps in the work of Glen Murcutt that we can see the most optimistic, hopeful expression of this practice in the Western world today. It is remarkable to see architecture and design executed with such skill on a technical level but even rarer to see it carried out in an unusual marriage of poetry with modernity.

Eric Owen Moss:
Junctions and Materials Made King

BELOW
With the full participation of his clients, Eric Owen Moss conceived Lawson–Westen House as a geometric dissecting of its elements: 'taking apart walls and ceiling; at the next scale down, doors and windows, and further still screws and washers, and reassembling them with a new geometry'. Seen here is the stairwell (opposite).

SURPRISE, experimentation with geometry, materials and their junctions: that is Eric Owen Moss (*b* 1943), a leading Californian architect whose buildings are more than just houses. Moss brings fresh and innovative ideas to domestic architecture. Ornament for him is the material itself, often that recognized as industrial, or non-domestic, such as concrete, plywood, rough sawn timber, rusted iron, galvanized steel. By bringing in materials that have strong textures, through unusual shapes and unexpected junctions, one begins to absorb some of his concern with 'otherness', a visible display of the workings of his creativity. There is relief in

the enjoyment of new ideas, a kind of freshness that is like a weight lifted from the dullness and inevitability of the familiar, the expected and the normal. His approach refreshes us and makes us feel more alive.

This is life at the cutting-edge, and it is not for everybody. It can prove uncomfortable because there is a shake-up of the familiar expectations of domesticity that exist within the northern European sensibility; comfort equates with cosiness, a substitute for dark, cold winters, and psychological protection in settlement patterns exposed historically to invasion and warfare. Contemporary, warm-climate California did not, and does not,

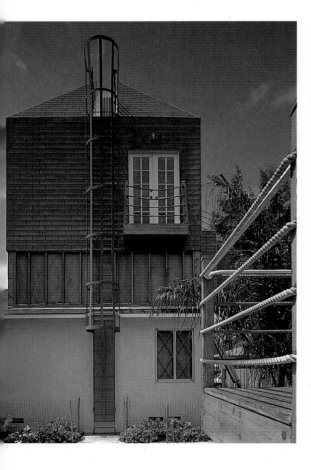

BELOW
Petal House, 1982–4, West Los Angeles. This external view shows how Moss makes the ordinary seem extraordinary. Pedestrian materials and familiar forms are used in a playful but contrived manner to create what he describes as 'emotive geometry'.

RIGHT
Main bedroom of the Lawson–Westen House. The position of the skylight provides well-balanced, indirect light in this highly sculpted room that nevertheless retains its traditional attic flavour. Living in such a challenging environment, beyond normal boundaries of domesticity, offers excitement but requires courage initially.

have those problems. And the range of materials now is not restricted to hand-cut timber and locally made bricks. Craft skills today are no longer related to expression in hand-carved stone, wood or the blacksmith. Central heating also releases us from the kitchen or fireplace circle, once the only usable space in winter in northern Europe. And, similarly, rooms no longer need to be small, or even conventionally seen as rooms at all. Perhaps they can be redefined as activity spaces, privacy zones or places for passing through – or as just giant live-in sculpture, where form, or the enjoyment of it, plays a major part: 'Living in Art' not just viewing it. The use of computer-generated forms, the development of twentieth-century sculpture with its immense freedom of composition, form and material must owe something to Moss's development. And why not? Perhaps this is ultimate interior design, where the space is the design, and where there is no difference between the furnishings and the walls, floors or ceiling in an attempt at philosophical unity? Is the ultimate interior design and architecture one in which they merge completely? There are others, but Moss's work certainly explores new boundaries in an exciting way.

In the Petal House (1982–4), West LA, a whole series of ideas interplay. There is Moss's enthusiasm for geometric games: 'emotive geometry', he calls it, where a conflict takes place among the hybrid of layers. First are the historical elements of a building, the normal expectations; these are then distorted and unravelled by a variety of means, particularly unexpected junctions and use of materials, which to some extent has been a modern Los Angeles tradition. But Moss takes it all further with his geometric gambles, through unexpected asymmetry in the roofline, position of windows, the hyperbolic rib system in the dining-room ceiling and the off-centre, curved entrance door. The original building required additions so the living room was pulled out, and a porch tucked on to the face of it. The window in the porch is the analogue of its counterpart in the living-room wall.

Lawson–Westen dining and living room. Although the playful sense of geometry is evident everywhere, here it creates spatial character, movement, diversity of scale and elements of domesticity. The fireplace retains its dominating role as the chief architectural feature of the living room.

Whether we want to live in such a challenging environment, where feelings of traditional domesticity have to be suspended, is another matter. But at least Moss offers a choice, where subliminal qualities such as bravery, courage and daring are being employed in the design, and there is an excitement about the whole enterprise, a moving forward with optimism, a push at the limits of possibility.

Out of necessity this causes discomfort, and the tolerance of such ideas is limited to those who are confident about their lifestyles and interested enough in design to bridge that gap between unfamiliarity and personal comfort as defined in the traditional northern European sense of home. It is particularly apt that this is happening in the USA. A preparedness to push towards new frontiers has always been part of American history, but often accompanied by, perhaps as compensation, a deep conservatism in home design among those who have been part of the great invention that is America. Eric Owen Moss provides the antithesis: a sense of adventure, reinvention and modernity.

Arquitectonica: *A Marriage of Rationality and Romanticism*

BELOW

Rational or romantic, Minimalist or committed to ornamental effect? All of these things, I suspect, and more. There is a positive enjoyment of ambiguity here.

ARQUITECTONICA have one of America's most exciting approaches to house design. Based in Miami, Florida, they are experimenting with the form of the house, pushing out the boundaries of what is conceivable, enjoyable and possible. The two main partners, Bernardo Fort-Brescia (*b* 1951) and Laurinda Spear (*b* 1951) bring their own individual energy and viewpoints to their work. Spear is more of an artist, being a painter in her own right, and Fort-Brescia is inclined towards architectural disciplines.

RIGHT

Sensual geometry; a chief passion of the two designers is used here to penetrate and explode, dominate and enhance built forms to create a character and atmosphere unique to each project. The chiefly defensive masonry walls are penetrated in tiny random openings with the exception of two circular windows.

They are married and have six children. At the core of their approach is the enjoyment of a dialogue between opposites, exemplified by their declaration as Modernists but with romantic leanings. They have built thoroughly well-engineered buildings that are offset by the unexpected or surreal. Geometry, their great passion, is utilized to penetrate and explode, distort and slice, dominate and enhance the internal and external built forms. Is it showmanship or engineering? High-tech or high jinx? Rational or romantic? This kind of ambiguity is enriching and ever present. It adds depth to the meaning and enjoyment of their architecture.

Although they have built more in the public domain – a series of enormous shopping malls and office blocks, their condominium high-rise, the Atlantis, is a famous Miami landmark through its inclusion in the opening sequence of the TV series *Miami Vice* – their one-off houses remain one of their most

Glazed elevation of the living room which, in direct contrast to the hall, is rather thin and lightweight. It is punctuated by heavily-framed structures – the fireplace and French door and window structures.

BELOW

Mulder House. In the evening the living room is lit to be dramatic and warmly welcoming. Privacy is ensured by the enclosed garden.

OPPOSITE

Mulder House. The living room viewed from the inside. The solidity and importance of the fireplace is emphasized by its position in a transparent wall. The impact and presence of the garden is strongly felt and links it in a manner similar to that of a conservatory.

exciting and favourite areas of work. The most interesting resolution of conflicting forces is the Mulder House (1983–5) in Lima, Peru. The house is divided into four quadrants, each with its own geometry, function and orientation. It is dominant, vigorous and fluid; logical, but with an air of whimsicality; preplanned but also sensual; strict but playful at the same time. Colour, texture and unexpected shapes perform throughout and aid connection to the garden, creating unexpected outside rooms, with the added bonus of extra privacy.

Indoors each quadrant has its own character and function that allows it to develop a strong atmosphere and individuality. There is enough character in the space to warrant simple furnishing. The first quadrant, the entrance hall, is defined by a rippled wall, the shape having qualities associated with fabric. Its narrow and textural qualities are enhanced cleverly by being punctuated with tiny square windows set at angles.

The second quadrant, formed as a partial ellipse, is the living room. Here a curtain-wall of floor-to-ceiling glass without mullions makes for a delicate and lightweight skin, to provide sensual elements in the envelope of the building. The third quadrant, spread over two floors, is the sleeping quarters. At the far end of it the library is separated by an exterior breezeway, thus providing a quiet and cool workplace.

The fourth quadrant is the service 'quarter' for the kitchen, laundry and so on. The dividing wall itself, although representative of the major planning idea, is not overplayed and is simply the more enjoyable for its sculptural qualities such as its narrowness, its cut-outs and its role as a backcloth to the drama of colour and shapes.

The Mulder House is a warm-climate house, and the living spaces are therefore airy, bright and unfussy. The modern design sits well in this context, but Arquitectonica have also designed for colder climates. Many of these former qualities prevail but with regional variations: for example the use of extending roof canopies, as in Prairie houses of Frank Lloyd Wright.

The Walner House (1985–7), near Lake Michigan, again shows the use of geometric forms as Arquitectonica's prime tool to articulate their work. A Z-plan was devised in response to the site, allowing access to three vistas and corresponding opportunities for outside spaces: a paved entry area, a grassy lawn, a view over the lake. Unexpected shapes of windows, controlled views, corridors, penetration of external light and a logical sequence of rooms, activities and views show the real gain of employing skilled designers, which is to be able to draw the most from the site, the climate and the building itself.

For those who think architects are unnecessary or self-absorbed stylists, or that Modernism is just a preoccupation with function, the work of Arquitectonica is living testimony that they are wrong. When the balance is struck right, then the pleasure of optimistic, individual, humane, rational and well-made modern architecture is real. It is a civilized and essential part of the present and the future.

Christopher Nevile:
Design Broker and Storyteller

INTERIOR design is a real skill, and although every house or apartment dweller assumes that mantle for themselves as a kind of automatically conferred prerogative, it isn't an innate skill and mostly needs to be earned. True we all have the right, and it is often necessary just to get the place furnished and to make it habitable as quickly as possible. But there is a distinction between a comfortable, sympathetic and visually satisfying environment that is a pleasure to use and an assemblage of one's chattels and appropriation of space based on need and a response to exigency. London-based Christopher Nevile (*b* 1954) is an interior designer and a broker of crafts and design. He enjoys assembling teams of skilled people to carry out interior-design projects, setting the visual and functional parameters. He offers refreshing insights and new ideas, and acts as a patron of the craft and design world through his shop, The Study, in Chelsea, encouraging new designers and those at the cutting-edge. Nevile's principal idea is that every room has to tell a story. This allows a certain thematic connection and helps provide continuity without being hidebound. It also involves wider themes that encourage diversity and experimentation. The results are more animated than sleek as well as being lively, irreverent and, perhaps sometimes, intentionally amateurish. His view is that interiors should be fun as well as functional.

After working in advertising and managing a graphic-design studio, Nevile trained as a specialist painter. As a result he has developed a disciplined eye with a great interest in surfaces and materials, the emotional impact of which, he believes, many people underestimate. When he first begins a project he builds up a picture or fantasy with the client of their ideal or imaginary interior, and then he pushes it a little to allow for potential inspiration, thus leaving a margin for input and discussion. He particularly enjoys orchestration, which gives him the opportunity to commission others to produce work for his projects. For example in the Mews House (1993), Lambeth, chairs, tables, mirrors and bedroom furniture were commissioned from contemporary craftspeople. In his own house the same geniality of spirit creates diversity and a sense of adventure. Each main piece of furniture ends up with a distinctiveness of its own. The dresser by Ray MacNeil is made from reused limed-oak and zinc, its roughness of texture thoroughly satisfying through the linkage of seaside grey-silver tones, offset by rope-pull handles. The punched aluminium bowl-light by Catherine Purves provides an element of whimsy with a handmade spontaneous quality that imbues the room with unusual surprise and delight.

Experiments and ideas abound in each room, often based on material, surface and colour but kept within the context of an overall story. His lack of formal design or architectural training allows Nevile to enjoy, focus and make

Canvas-covered walls of Chris Nevile's own garden room, painted by Fiona Sutcliffe to give a witty interpretation of an informal garden–dining room. A quiet send-up of Rococo elegance and chinoiserie creates a polite, but comfortable room, through Mad Hatterish details. The overscaled chairs by Nevile himself double up as chaises-longues.

use of these elements with great freedom. He is less hamstrung by design and spatial theory and more interested in the cybernetic qualities awaiting exploitation by the intelligent use of shapes, colours and textures. Given his belief in the emotional content in these elements, there is tremendous scope for de-emotionalizing clients' decision-making. With so many emotionally rich objects, from antiques to work by contemporary craftspeople, from which to choose when creating an interior, this is a necessary role for a designer to offer. Providing a rational basis with logical connections and an outsider's view can be vital.

With the build-up of skill through practice and study Nevile offers such observations as: 'Broken colour softens walls, while it crispens objects in the room.' Rigorous architecture and cabinetry can flatten this, and he believes old buildings offer us clues. He enjoys the ambience and richness found in old country houses, where bad taste comes into play with inherited items, pragmatic shortcuts, the differing tastes of successive generations, the effects of age and the patina of use, which all combine to make a layer of visual history that is both unassumed and satisfyingly rich at the same time. The enjoyment of objects in their own right involves understanding the story behind them, and in English country houses the role of patronage was vital. Our ancestors chose the work of those individual artists, designers and craftspeople that they valued and understood, and these houses have become a controlled assemblage of the top artisans and designers of their time. In some respects Christopher Nevile acts in a similar way, but as a service for his clients, rather than himself, and to standards that many admire and appreciate.

A beautiful fireplace which challenges conventional design disciplines by subjecting a strongly classical Georgian block composition, with its formal keystone centrepiece, to a rough construction created in hand-sawn logs – particularly suitable for a wood burning fireplace. The design shown here was master-minded by Justin Meath-Baker.

Charles Rutherfoord:
Understated Innovation

BELOW
In this small flat in London's Mayfair Rutherfoord creates ambience mainly through his heightened sense of colour and texture. Few understand how to create richness without resorting to an overstated use of pattern or unnecessary decoration. The aperture for flowers adds an instant touch of grandeur crossed with domesticity.

I T would be too easy to dismiss British architect Charles Rutherfoord (*b* 1956) as no more than a humane and intelligent Modernist. But his training includes a qualification in architectural history and three years working for Christie's auction house, valuing and cataloguing eighteenth-century English furniture. With his degree in Interior Design and earlier architectural training, he has accommodated an almost perfect combination of skills for domestic interior design, similar to those I call for in the introduction to this section. In essence his talent combines interior architecture, a knowledge of the exterior envelope with an ability to design furniture.

RIGHT
Experimentation, in the kitchen of the same apartment, with new combinations of materials. A polyester work-top, plasticized fireproof counter curtains, a patinated copper wall and extractor fan, all decked out in rich but compatible colours, make this room simultaneously easy to live with and glamorous.

Ultimately what is important is not only the absorption of design skills *per se* but also how they are applied. It is the poetry in a designer's work, what is beyond the merely functional, that shows the necessary vitality and humanity that provide the opportunity for sheer enjoyment of interiors. We take it for granted that the mechanics, the practical day-to-day usability will be worked out, but it is that extra element, not so much how to deal in a textbook fashion with unexpected hitches as the use of ingenuity to enhance the hidden agenda of ambience and elegance that invigorate the solution. I mean by this a sense of an unexpected wholeness, a surprising holistic quality that is not only logical but contains a capacity for surprise and fun at the same time. It avoids overblown whimsicality but includes a quiet and confident inventiveness that infuses it with imagination and sensuality. This is what differentiates Charles Rutherfoord's work from that of some other contemporary designers and provides the freshness in his work.

Examining Rutherfoord's technique in more detail it is possible to see his skills as existing in several separate but connected layers. There is his use of colour and textures, his unexpected mix of material, and his capacity to put together new combinations, especially in his furniture, and employ daring shapes. For example, his design of, say, an armchair is along conventional lines

These highly inventive furniture designs have diverse creative origins, but, as a collection, they work well together. Charles Rutherfoord enjoys both decoration and simplicity, austerity and richness. This makes for interesting and exotic combinations and allows the development of an original repertoire.

171

In this study area of the Mayfair flat the horizontal linen Roman blind provides an interesting contrast to the highly polished plaster surface of the rippled dividing wall.

but made distinct by the uniqueness of the Siamese twin-feature, while his feeling for texture and colour is paramount.

Rutherfoord mostly works as an interior designer with architectural ambitions that are followed by his enthusiasm for furniture design. In his first house (1986) in Hillgate Place for a London banker, he was way ahead of his time in his mix and use of materials. Interested in their innate qualities, not just as a managed surface, he used cast concrete, raw polished plaster, natural stone juxtaposed with wooden floors and no extraneous detail. The richness was in the materials, not so much in their shape or detail as in their junctions and meaning. His mentor at this stage was Carlo Scarpa, the renowned late Italian Modernist architect, who has similar attitudes to his materials. There is a lot of wisdom in this, because a lack of respect for inherent qualities in materials is undoubtedly a hallmark of indifferent architecture and interior design. It is a sign of maturity, sensibility and skill to utilize materials in a considered yet simple way that can produce a sense of completeness. This, in turn, is one of the qualities associated with both minimalism and Modernism. The downside is that carried to the extreme it can lead to a certain harshness and lack of humanity, especially in domestic interiors. This can upset our nesting instincts or the homely qualities that are also an aspect of domesticity. Balance is, of course, what is needed.

Rutherfoord's work has moved on from his earlier more formal and rational use of materials to easier, warmer and more tactile choices. Although this might be expected in more relaxed spaces such as the living room, with its penchant for soft fabrics, nevertheless he selects curtains and sofa covers to form a key element in the overall materials mix as well as a softer design for the bookshelves and special provision of a place for flowers, a clear sign of both domesticity and femininity. Equally there is an harmonious absorption of antique furniture and bric-à-brac. This all signals a melting in attitude from hard-nosed modernity to an increased enjoyment of the old and familiar. In more hardworking rooms such as the kitchen, where the fabric is more rugged, the result has a decidedly domestic element to it. Bright colours are apparent in the resin-coated work-top and an aged copper on the wall behind, and other metallic finishes add a touch of warmth. Even the bathroom in the house (1987) in South Kensington, which needed the most hard-wearing surfaces of all, has a curved mosaic-covered wall, wooden floors and stainless-steel appliances with a long wall of mirrors to increase light levels, all giving a humane balance of finishes. This is sensitive and imaginative Modernism, easy to live with and enjoyable to use.

For Charles Rutherfoord comfort is not so much a coy set of visual domestic references, such as mantelpiece ornaments or lush armchairs, as the provision of an environment that is a pleasure to use; for him, something that is inconvenient or does not work well is uncomfortable. He may like me to add that his definition of comfort and modernity includes less quantifiable ingredients, such as wit, elegance and colour, qualities that every home needs, in addition to the other qualites of a hardworking house.

In this confined Mayfair dining area Rutherfoord has used curved walls to create a specific eating area linked to the shape of the table. The patterned hanging tube is a light.

ABOVE
This bathroom in a private house in London, was another spatial challenge. With the aid of careful design, an original, but visually sustaining choice of material plus the use of mirrors, the room remains elegant despite the dominance of the large window and shower enclosure, dividing up the original single room without causing too much disruption.

BIBLIOGRAPHY

Alexander, Christopher: *A Pattern of Language* (Oxford University Press, 1977)

American Builders' Companion (1806)

Austen, Jane: *Sense and Sensibility* (1811)

Beecher, Catherine: *A Treatise on Domestic Economy* (1849)

Carter, David: *Psychology for Architects* (Linden Applied Science Publishers, 1974)

Cecil, David: *A Portrait of Jane Austen* (Constable, London, 1978)

Country Builders' Assistant (1797)

Cruickshank, Dan: *The Name of the Room* (BBC Books, London, 1993)

Davey, Peter: *Arts and Crafts Architecture* (Phaidon Press, London, 1995)

Douglas, Mary, and Isherwood, Baron: *World of Goods: Towards an Anthropology of Consumption* (Allen Lane, London, 1978)

Douglas, Mary: *Purity and Danger* (Routledge, London, 1966)

Garrett, Wendell: *American Colonial* (Cassell, London, 1995)

Gill, Brendan: *Many Masks* (Heinemann, London, 1987)

Grey, Johnny: *The Art of Kitchen Design* (Cassell, London, 1994)

Grey, Johnny: 'In Place of Modernism', *Design Magazine*, no. 390, June 1981, pp.53–4

Handy, Charles: *The Empty Raincoat* (Hutchinson, London, 1994)

Hughes, Robert: *The Shock of the New* (Thames & Hudson, London, 1991)

Italy: The New Domestic Landscape (exh. cat. Museum of Modern Art, New York, 1972)

Jung, C.G.: *Memories, Dreams, Reflections*, ed. Aniela Jaffé (New York and London, 1963)

Kelly, Kevin: *Out of Control: The New Biology of Machines* (Fourth Estate, London, 1994)

Kron, Joan: *Home Psyche*, (Potter, New York, 1983)

Marc, Oliver: *The Psychology of the House* (Thames & Hudson, London, 1971)

Maslow, Abraham: *Motivation and Personality* (Harper and Row, London, 1954)

Ruskin, John: *The Seven Lamps of Architecture* (Dent & Dutton, London, 1956)

Schama, Simon: *The Embarrassment of Riches* (Fontana Press, London, 1987)

Sprigg, June, and Larkin, David: *Shaker Life, Work and Art* (Cassell, London, 1987)

Sweeney, James, and Sert, Josep Luis: *Antonio Gaudí* (Architectural Press, 1960)

Trevelyan, G.M.: *An Illustrated English Social History*, vol. 2 (Pelican, London, 1952)

Walters, Derek: *The Feng Shui Handbook* (Aquarian Press, 1991)

Webb, Michael: *Architects House Themselves* (Preservation Press, Washington D.C., 1991)

Wilson, Colin: *The Occult* (Granada, London, 1978)

Yagi, Koji: *A Japanese Touch for Your Home* (Kodansha International, Tokyo, 1982)

PHOTOGRAPHIC ACKNOWLEDGEMENTS

Arcaid/Richard Bryant 8, 11, 24, 68(b), 69/**Jeremy Cockayne** 16, 27/**Julie Phipps** 160/**Lucinda Lambton** 26, 28, 29, 49, 104(t)/**John Edward Linden** 35/**Ken Kirkwood** 42(b), 127/**Farrell Grehan** 66/**Martin Jones** 73/ E Stoller/Esto 77/**Bill Tingey** 79(b)/**Dennis Gilbert** 135. **Architectural Association** 72(1), 75, 76(r).**Tom Bonner** 22, 150, 158, 159, 160(r). **Bridgeman Art Library/Mallet & Son Antiques Ltd.**, **London** 43/**Private Collecton** 50, 100/**Agnew & Sons, London** 87/**Forbes Magazine Collection**, **New York** 116/**Stapleton Collection** 128, 134/**Christies Images** 144. **Martin Charles** 60, 62, 63, 67, 68(t), 72(r). **Jerome Darblay** 173(r). **Mark Darley** 12, 17, 84, 93(1&r) 94, 95, 138. **Edifice/Lewis** 53, 74/**Darley** 80, 83. **Esto/Scott Francis** 21, 161. **Michael Freeman** 32(t), 46, 54, 55, 56(b), 57, 58, 59(1&r), 81. **Tim Goffe** 169(t&b). **Johnny Grey** (all plans) 4, 100(t&b), 101, 102, 105, 108, 112(1), 123(t), 130(t&b), 133, 136, 137,139(t,b&r), 140, 147, 149. **Johnny Grey** 14, l9(t), 23, 25, 45, 82(l), 96(1&r), 97(1&r), 98(t&b), 99(t&b), 103, 117, 119, 122, 123(b), 124, 131(t&b), 132(1&r), 145(t&b), 146, 147. **Robert Harding Syndication/Country Homes & Interiors/Tim Goffe** 32(b), 56(t), 111(b), 166, 167, 168. **Ryo Hata** 76(1), 78, 82(r).**Tim Hursley** 153(t), 162(1&r), 163, 164, 165. **Interior Archive/Simon Brown** 169. **Grey Crawford** 37. **Tom Layton** 34, 36, 170(1&r), 171, 172, 173(1). **Life magazine** 39. **James Mortimer** 1, 2, 3, 10, 13, 30, 42(t), 48, 51, 86, 89, 90, 91, 92, 104(b), 106(t&b), 107, 111(t), 112(r), 113(t&b), 115, 118, 121 (t,b&r), 125, 126, 129. **Rhiner Bloch** 153(b), 154(b), 155, 156, 157. **National Trust Photographic Library/Bill Batten** 52, 120/**Michael Caldwell** 61/**Jonathan Gibson** 70. **Oki Doki** 154(t). **Tiggy Ruthven** 64, 65. **S C Ward** 18. **Elizabeth Whiting & Associates** 9/**Michael Nicholson** 20/**Brian Harrison** 33/**Frank Herholdt** 38/**Neil Lorimer** 39, 41/**Clive Helm** 40/**Spike Powell** 44/**Tim Street Porter** 109/**Peter Woloszynski** 141/**Jean-Paul Bonhommet** 142.

INDEX